Dear Anne & ~~Sharon~~ ZOLTAN

We wish to thank you
for joining us at the
41st Annual Dinner of the

Young Israel of Forest Hills.

It is wonderful to share
this occasion with our friends.

MARION & HANS

MAN OF FAITH IN THE MODERN WORLD

REFLECTIONS OF THE RAV

VOLUME TWO

MAN OF FAITH IN THE MODERN WORLD

REFLECTIONS OF THE RAV
VOLUME TWO

adapted from lectures of

RABBI JOSEPH B. SOLOVEITCHIK

by

RABBI ABRAHAM R. BESDIN

KTAV PUBLISHING HOUSE, INC.
HOBOKEN, NEW JERSEY
1989

The support of the Memorial Foundation for Jewish Culture is gratefully acknowledged.

Copyright © 1989
Abraham R. Besdin and Joseph B. Soloveitchik

Library of Congress Cataloging-in-Publication Data

Besdin, Abraham R.
    Reflections of the Rav / adapted from lectures of Joseph B. Soloveitchik by Abraham R. Besdin.
      p. cm.
    Includes index.
    Contents: v. 2. Man of faith in the modern world
    ISBN 0-88125-312-X (v. 2)
    1. Judaism.   I. Soloveitchik, Joseph Dov.   II. Title.
BM45.B47   1989
296—dc19   89-30895
                                                                                 CIP

Manufactured in the United States of America

CONTENTS

Preface	9
Abbreviations	13

Transmitting the Mesorah

I	The First Jewish Grandfather	15
II	Symbolism of Blue and White	25

The Lonely Man of Faith

III	The Man of Faith in a Technological World, Part I	36
IV	The Man of Faith in a Technological World, Part II	46

The Ideal Marriage

V	As a Bridegroom with His Bride	56

Patriarchal Lessons

VI	Shaping Jewish Character	66
VII	Destiny, Not Causality, Governs Jewish History	70
VIII	The Universal and the Covenantal	73
IX	The Covenantal Role of Sarah	83

Rationalizing Mitzvot

X	May We Interpret Ḥukim?	91
XI	Interpreting the Parah Adumah	100

Triumph in Sorrow

XII	From Negation to Affirmation	117
XIII	Sitting Shivah Is Doing Teshuvah	125

6 / *Man of Faith in the Modern World*

Rosh Hashanah, Yom Kippur, Sukkot

XIV	Rabbi Akiba's Homily on Teshuvah	133
XV	The Haftarah of Jonah on Yom Kippur	141
XVI	Hakafot—Moving in Circles	150

Index 161

למזכרת עולם

"כבד את אביך ואת אמך" (שמות כ, יב)
ו' יתירה, לרבות אחיך הגדול (כתובות קג)

מוקדש לזכרו הטהור של אחי האהוב
ר' אליהו חיים בה"ר אליעזר צבי בית-דין ז"ל
נפ' י"ג אלול תשד"מ

"הולך תמים ופועל צדק ודבר אמת בלבבו" (תהלים טו, ב)

It is with loving tribute
that I dedicate this volume
to the memory of my worthy brother

Herman E. Besdin ז"ל

the *bekhor* of our family,
who was *niftar* on
September 10, 1984 / 13 Elul 5744

*"He walked uprightly and acted righteously,
and spoke truth with his heart"* (*Psalms 15:2*)

תנצב"ה

Tishre 5749

PREFACE

לזרעך נתתי את הארץ הזאת, מנהר מצרים עד הנהר הגדול, נהר פרת
(בראשית טו, יח)
פי' רש"י — "הנהר הגדול" — לפי שהוא דבוק לארץ ישראל, קוראהו גדול
. . . משל הדיוט: עבד מלך מלך. הדבק לשחוור וישתחוו לך (שבועות מז, ב).

> *To your descendants I have given this land, from the Egyptian river as far as the great river, the Euphrates (Genesis 15:18).*
> *Rashi: "the great river"—Because it is mentioned in connection with the land of Israel, Scripture calls it "great." [Although it is the last mentioned of the four rivers that went out of Eden (2:14).] There is a popular proverb: "A king's servant is a king; attach yourself to a captain and people will bow down to you!"*

The worldwide acceptance of *Reflections of the Rav,* published in 1979, and its Hebrew edition, *P'rakim B'Mahshevet Harav,* in 1984, has emboldened me to prepare this sequel. I acknowledge my role, in the words of Rashi, as that of a "servant of the king." The bows of recognition which have come my way are truly intended for the Rav, the "captain" who has guided my Torah *hashkafah* during my adult lifetime. It is with trepidation, but also with feelings of rare privilege, that I am bringing this second volume to public attention.

Harav Soloveitchik was born in Poland in 1903 to a family noted for outstanding Torah scholarship. His grandfather, Rav Chaim of Brisk, and his father, Rav Moshe, had revitalized Talmudic study through a renewed emphasis on scientific clarification and rigorous analysis. He also pursued his secular studies at the University of Berlin, where he concentrated on logic and metaphysics, and was awarded a Ph.D. degree in 1931.

Arriving in the United States in 1932, he settled in Boston, where he guided the development of the Maimonides Day School. In 1941 he succeeded his father as *Rosh Yeshivah* at the Yeshivat Rabbenu Yitzchak Elchanan of Yeshiva University and was also appointed Professor of Philosophy at its Graduate Schools.

Besides his regular *shiurim* at the Yeshiva, he drew thousands of scholars, students, and common folks to his two annual *shiurim*—the *Yahrzeit Shiur,* in memory of his father, and the *Teshuvah Shiur,* during the Ten Days of Repentance. In addition, there were weekly *shiurim* open to the public in mid-Manhattan and in Boston which attracted many university students.

The Rav, as he is reverently known to his *talmidim* and admirers, has achieved world renown for his mastery of Halakhah and Aggadah. His halakhic *shiurim* are acknowledged as unsurpassed in their breadth of knowledge and analytical depth. He is also a brilliant expositor of Aggadah. The Rav holds large audiences spellbound as he weaves together insights from the Talmud, Midrash, Kabbalah, and contemporary sources. The versatility of his knowledge and the freshness of understanding he brings to most subjects are widely recognized in scholarly and lay circles. In addition, the Rav is endowed with a charismatic personality and a dramatic eloquence which invest his talks with the compelling power of a unique experience.

My primary objective in composing these texts is to make the salient ideas of the Rav's *hashkafah* more widely available. These essays are not literal transcriptions of the Rav's presentations. Rather, they are reconstructions in which texts, ideas, often in the Rav's own felicitous language, are organized and formulated in a manner suitable for the general reader. I have at all times been aware of the awesome responsibility to preserve the authenticity of the Rav's ideas. I caution the reader that all weaknesses in the text, whether stylistic or substantive, are to be ascribed solely to my faulty transmission and interpretation. I pray that such instances are minor and infrequent.

I would like to express my gratitude to those who assisted me in bringing this volume to fruition.

To Rabbi Menachem Genack, a *talmid muvhak* of the Rav and the Rabbinic Administrator of the Orthodox Union, for meticulously reviewing the entire manuscript, offering many valuable suggestions; and to Mr. Julius Berman for his sage counsel and unfailing helpfulness.

And I acknowledge, with gratitude to the Almighty, my *Ayshet Ḥayil,* Elana, whose persistent encouragement was greatly responsible for my perseverance in completing this work. We thank God for our children, Adeena Lee, Hillel and Bonnie, and Alisa Miriam, and our grandchildren, Yosef Mendel and Rivka Rochel. We pray that we may be blessed "to see our children and children's children occupied with Torah and *mitzvot.*"

Tishre 5749   *Abraham R. Besdin*

ABBREVIATIONS

Note.—"Gen. R.", "Ex. R.", etc. indicates *Midrash Rabbah* commentary.

Biblical References

Gen.	Genesis
Ex.	Exodus
Lev.	Leviticus
Num.	Numbers
Deut.	Deuteronomy
Judg.	Judges
Josh.	Joshua
Sam.	Samuel
Isa.	Isaiah
Jer.	Jeremiah
Ezek.	Ezekiel
Mic.	Micah
Hab.	Habakkuk
Zech.	Zechariah
Mal.	Malachi
Ps.	Psalms
Prov.	Proverbs
Eccles.	Ecclesiastes
Esth.	Esther
Chron.	Chronicles

Talmudic References

Ber.	Berakhot
Shab.	Shabbat
Pes.	Pesahim
Ta'an.	Sukkah Ta'anit
Meg.	Megillah
M.K.	Mo'ed Katan
Yev.	Yevamot
Ket.	Ketubbot
Git.	Gittin
Kid.	Kiddushin
B. Kam.	Bava Kama
B. Metz.	Bava Metzia
B. Bat.	Bava Batra
Sanh.	Sanhedrin
Mak.	Makkot
Ed.	Eduyyot
Av.	Avot
A.Z.	Avodah Zarah
Men.	Menahot
Tem.	Temurah
Nid.	Niddah

Chapter I

THE FIRST JEWISH GRANDFATHER

A Child Is Born

A grandfather stands before his newly born grandchild filled with paradoxical thoughts. Feelings of renewal merge with fading memories of the past. For the Torah-committed Jew, this scene has an added dimension. Gazing at the newborn, the grandfather also experiences a sense of "generation awareness." What is "generation awareness"?

Grandfathers and grandchildren, though members of different generations, are part of one fraternity—the *Mesorah* community (those who preserve the integrity of the transmitted tradition). Just prior to his death, Moses told the Israelites, "I make this covenant and this oath not with you alone, but with those who are standing here with us this day before the Lord our God, and with those who are not with us this day" (Rashi: "also with future generations") (Deut. 29:13–14).[1] Jews of the past, present, and future are united in their commitment to the Divine teachings of the Torah and to the historical destiny of the Jew. One collegial fraternity exists of Moses, Rabbi Akiba, Maimonides, the Gaon of Vilna, the Besht, and others, joining hands with grandfathers, parents, and children of all generations.

As the child is born, he is absorbed into the *Mesorah* community. He will, hopefully, speak our language, study our texts, share our solemnities, dream our dreams, and adopt our ideals. Rashi will be his lifelong companion in Torah study, as he is ours. In this fraternity of the committed, there need not be any generation gap, any splintering of ranks, but rather a sharing of ideas and ideals which span and unite countless generations. Each newborn child enters an extended historical family where he will be reared by the wisdom and teachings of great Torah personalities, all interested in his spiritual awakening and development.

When it is achieved, a *Mesorah* relationship between grandfather and grandchild contains an emotional intensity and intellectual closeness that in some ways transcends the parent-child relationship. Psychologically, one would not expect a deep identification between two individuals whose great discrepancy of years could easily spawn alienation. Yet grandparents, more so than parents, are sensitive to the transiency of time and to the pressing need to assure the perpetuation of one's lifelong principles. The child is far more than a biological extension; he embodies one's hopes for spiritual continuity. If, as is found frequently, a bond between old and young is achieved amongst Torah Jews, it is due to this singular awareness of a *Mesorah* community in which past and present generations are contemporaries. Distance in time is bridged, and divergence in outward style is rendered irrelevant. This is in sharp contrast to the secular scene, where generations too often confront each other as cultural antagonists.

The Secret of Uniting Generations

So unique is this "generation-awareness" to the Jew that Rabbi Akiba declared it to be a major factor in bringing about the eschatological fulfillment of A*ḥ*rit ha-yamim, the ultimate redemption of the Jewish people.

Rabbi Akiba states: A father endows his son with comely appearance, strength, riches, wisdom, longevity, and *mispar hadorot lefanov,* the number of generations (that had been his progenitors) before him. And *v'hu haketz,* this is (the secret of) the redemption, as it says: "He proclaimed the generations from the beginning" [Isa. 41:4] (Ed. 2:9).[2]

There is no doubt that the genetic codes of the parents and the conditions of the home environment affect a child's physical, intellectual, and economic status. But what is *mispar hadorot lefanav,* whose transmission Rabbi Akiba says will bring redemption to our people?

This enigmatic statement has been variously interpreted by Talmudic commentators. We believe that Rabbi Akiba, speaking in the chaotic, strife-torn Bar Kochba period (circa 135 C.E.), was setting forth the premise of Jewish survival, namely, the ability of parents to transmit to their children the secret of uniting with past generations, of whatever number, dating back to antiquity. It is the ability to associate with distant historical figures, intellectually and emotionally, as if they were contemporary companions. Intergenerational dialogues become feasible as lines of communication are established, defying barriers of time and circumstance. If a grandfather can bridge this gap with his grandchild because they are fraternal brothers in a spiritual association, then this breakthrough is also possible with great-grandparents and great-great- grandparents even if they are long deceased.

The possibilities of identifying with our ancestors are endless, boundless, and can reach back to our earliest history. He who can "proclaim (an identity with) the generations from the beginning," will help bring about the eschatological fulfillment of *aḥrit ha-yamim,* the redemption and vindication of the Jewish people.

The First Grandfather

We have three patriarchs: Abraham, Isaac, and Jacob. Our history, however, has bestowed upon Jacob two prerogatives which were denied to the earlier patriarchs. First, the names Jacob and Israel became the generic names for the entire people as such. Moses was frequently commanded to "speak to the children of Israel," and Isaiah proclaimed, "O house of Jacob, come, let us walk by the light of the Lord" (2:5). Abraham and Isaac remained individual names which were never raised to the

18 / *Man of Faith in the Modern World*

level of a collective group name. Only Jacob was so honored.

A second distinction is that Jacob is frequently called "the old one" *(zaken)* in the Torah and the Midrash, despite the fact that Abraham and Isaac lived longer.[3] He never achieved their longevity. When Jacob refused to let Banjamin return to Egypt with his brothers, Judah said, "Leave the old man alone until the house runs short of bread (and Jacob will then be forced to change his mind)" (Rashi, Gen. 43:2).[4] Later on, Joseph asks, "Is your old father, *avikhem hazaken,* about whom you speak, at peace? Is he yet alive?" (43:27). Maimonides, explaining the source of the prayer, *Barukh shem kevod malkhuto lo-olam vaed,* "Blessed he His glorious majesty forever and ever," which follows the opening verse of the Shema Yisrael, writes: "*Pasaḥ hazaken v'amar,* the 'old one' exclaimed it after being reassured of the piety of his children (Pes. 56a). Therefore it is a custom in Israel to recite the praise which the 'old Israel,' *Yisrael hazaken,* said after the Shema"(Hil. Kriyat Shema 1:4).[5] The appellation *zaken* is used without mentioning his name, it being understood that the reference is to Jacob.[6]

In Talmudic and Midrashic literature, Jacob is often called *Yisrael Sava,* "Old Israel," and this term, too, is employed even in modern usage, to designate Jews who observe the old tradition.[6] In what manner, we ask, did Jacob distinguish himself, that his name became the generic name for an entire people, and why is he, in particular, called the *Zaken?*

The answer is that Jacob was the first patriarch to establish direct communication with his grandchildren. He was the first to make a solemn declaration, an historic pronouncement, which is responsible for the sense of closeness we still have with the past, thereby laying the foundation for the dialogue of the generations. He literally conquered time and space when he said to Joseph, "Now your two sons, who were born to you in the land of Egypt, before I came to you in Egypt, are mine. Ephraim and Menashe shall be mine, no less than Reuben and Simeon" (Gen. 48:5).[7] In fact, they received portions in the later division of the Holy Land, as did the sons of Israel (Rashi).

Though a second generation removed, and nurtured in an Egyptian environment, Jacob equated them with his own sons who had been reared close to him in the Holy Land.

Abraham never spoke this way about Jacob, that he was to him as Isaac. Isaac never said it about Reuben and Simeon. Jacob was the first to impart special blessings to his grandchildren, "The angel who redeemed me from all harm, may he bless these lads" (v. 16).[8] He blessed them even before he assembled his own sons for their blessings. He embraced them between his knees, and he placed his hands upon their heads. This signified, symbolically, that there was a direct transmission from Jacob to Ephraim and Menashe. There was no generation gap in the house of Jacob. The halakhic ruling that *b'nai banim harei hem k'banim,* "grandchildren have the same status as children" (Yev. 62b), is derived from Jacob's declaration about Ephraim and Menashe.[9]

Abraham and Isaac transmitted their spiritual heritage to their sons, not to their grandsons. The latter received it from their fathers, but there was no direct communication between Abraham and Jacob or between Isaac and Reuben and Simeon. The influence of the grandfathers on their grandchildren was indirect. Jacob, however, related directly to his grandchildren; he did not need an intermediary or an interpreter; his was a direct dialogue. He leapt over the gulf of generations and transmitted the great *Mesorah* of Abraham directly to Ephraim and Menashe. Despite the discrepancy of years, the *Zaken,* the carrier of the old tradition, succeeded.

How appropriate, therefore, that our people is called Israel or Jacob, for it was he who created the Jewish community which ensures Jewish continuity. What preceded him were patriarchal families. He laid the foundation for a people. Though the covenant was made initially with Abraham, it was not until Jacob that the secret of perpetuating the *Mesorah* was discovered.

The Midrash tells that the sons of Joseph studied with their grandfather daily after his arrival in Egypt (Rashi, Gen. 48:1;

Tanḥuma Va'yeḥi).[10] It was the *Zaken* who listened to their problems, conversed and worked closely with them, played and planned with them. The most effective teacher is not he who lectures his students with detachment, but rather he who befriends his disciples, and together they become co-searchers and co-dreamers in the pursuit of truth. Jacob knew the secret language of *mispar hadorot,* of uniting generations. Some can do it, and, unfortunately, many others, even noted scholars, who are intelligent and inspired leaders, cannot bridge the generation gap. The parent, grandparent, or teacher who sensitizes a child to his antecedents is the guarantor of the survival of the *Mesorah.*

Living in Retrospection

Contemporary man is so proud of his technological achievements that he has contempt for the past. His pride in progress makes him reject introspection. The man in the street has little relationship with and consciousness of continuity and interdependency between glorious periods of antiquity and the emerging present. Even medieval and modern history, from which not many years separate us, appears mythical, romantic, and elusive.

The Jew of the *Mesorah,* however, has a capacity to live in retrospection. Revelation and tradition erase the bounds of time. Distance in time is rendered irrelevant for him. Thousands of years have elapsed, but he walks back and forth from antiquity to modern times. The primary success of the old *ḥeder* (the old fashioned one room religious elementary school), although deficient in many respects, lay in this spirit of compenetration of a distant past and a dim future with the immediate present.

For Jewish boys and girls, Abraham is not a mythical figure, but an ever-present inspiration. They experience his tribulations and wanderings. They travel with him from Syria to Canaan. They feel the fear and trembling of Isaac during the *Akedah.*

They escape with Jacob to Haran. They are imprisoned with Joseph in the pit and rejoice in his ascent to high office and fame. They lead the Jews with Moses through the desert of Sinai. They sing with David and are exalted by the prophets. They eagerly join the rebellion against Rome with Rabbi Akiba and mourn the tragedy which befell his twenty-four-thousand students. They meditate with the Rambam and are privileged to have Rashi as a companion in the study of *Humash* (Pentateuch). These figures are not dead or historical "has-beens" but dynamic, living heroes who visit us from time to time, bringing instruction, inspiration, and hope.

Upon this phenomenon of an historical continuum was founded the strength of the *Mesorah,* conceived as an historic stream of Jewish spirit whose tributaries of past, present, and future merge into each other.

It is this ability to span the generations that explains the impassioned solidarity of American and world Jewry with the struggle of the State of Israel. Why should a Jew in New York or Chicago, who never saw Eretz Yisrael and had heard little about it in earlier years, be so committed to its welfare and preservation? Apparently, the Jews who lived in the Holy Land nineteen hundred years ago, Rabbi Yohanan ben Zakkai and the heroes of Masada and Betar, are somehow communicating with us today, and the antenna of the Jew is uniquely sensitive and receptive to distant signals. The lines of transmission are not always clear, but the message has been getting through.

The Experience of a Rosh Yeshiva

The old Rebbe walks into the classroom crowded with students who are young enough to be his grandchildren.* He enters as an old man with wrinkled face, his eyes reflecting the fatigue and sadness of old age. (This pensiveness, typical of old age, emerges out of an awareness of people and things which are

---
*The incident described in this section was represented by the Rav as his personal experience.

rapidly disappearing, which linger only in memory.) The Rebbe is seated and sees before him rows of young beaming faces, clear eyes radiating the joy of being young. For a moment, the Rebbe is gripped with pessimism, with tremors of uncertainty. He asks himself, "Can there be a dialogue between an old teacher and young students, between a Rebbe in his Indian summer and students enjoying the spring of their lives?" The Rebbe starts the *shiur,* uncertain as to how it will proceed.

Suddenly, the door opens and an old man, much older than the Rebbe, enters. He is the grandfather of the Rebbe, Reb Chaim Brisker (1853–1918). It would be most difficult to study Talmud with students who are trained in the sciences and mathematics, were it not for his method, which is very modern and equals, if not surpasses, most contemporary forms of logic, metaphysics, or philosophy.

The door opens again and another old man comes in. He is older than Reb Chaim, for he lived in the seventeenth century. His name is Reb Sabbatai Cohen (1622–1663), known as the *Shakh,* who must be present when civil law, *dinei mamonot,* is discussed. Many more visitors arrive, some from the eleventh, twelfth, and thirteenth centuries, and others harking back to antiquity—Rabbenu Tam (1090–1171), Rashi (1040–1105), Rambam (1135–1204), Rabad (1125–1198), Rashba (1245–1310), Rabbi Akiba (40–135), and others. These scholarly giants of the past are bidden to take their seats.

The Rebbe introduces the guests to his pupils, and the dialogue commences. The Rambam states a halakhah; the Rabad disagrees sharply, as is his wont. Some students interrupt to defend the Rambam, and they express themselves harshly against the Rabad, as young people are apt to do. The Rebbe softly corrects the students and suggests more restrained tones. The Rashba smiles gently. The Rebbe tries to analyze what the students meant, and other students intercede. Rabbenu Tam is called upon to express his opinion, and, suddenly, a symposium of generations comes into existence. Young students debate earlier generations with an air of daring familiarity, and a crescendo of discussion ensues.

All speak one language; all pursue one goal; all are committed to a common vision; and all operate with the same categories. A *Mesorah* collegiality is achieved, a friendship, a comradeship of old and young, spanning antiquity, the Middle Ages, and modern times. *V'hu haketz,* this joining of the generations, this merger of identities will ultimately bring about the redemption of the Jewish people. It will fulfill the words of the last of the Hebrew prophets, Malachi, "And he [Elijah] shall turn the heart of the fathers to the children and the heart of the children to their fathers" (3:24).[11] The Messianic realization will witness the great dialogue of the generations.

After a two- or three-hour *shiur,* the Rebbe emerges from the chamber young and rejuvenated. He has defeated age. The students look exhausted. In the *Mesorah* experience, years play no role. Hands, however parchment-dry and wrinkled, embrace warm and supple hands in a commonality, bridging the gap which separates the generations.

Thus, the "old ones" of the past continue their great dialogue of the generations, ensuring an enduring commitment to the *Mesorah. V'hu haketz*—this is the secret that will lead to the Messianic redemption.

הערות לפרק 1

1 **דברים כט, יג-יד:** ולא אתכם לבדכם אנכי כרת את הברית הזאת ואת האלה הזאת, כי את אשר ישנו פה עמנו עומד היום לפני ה' אלקינו, ואת אשר איננו פה עמנו היום: פי' רש"י — ואף עם דורות העתידין להיות.

2 **משנה עדיות פ"ב מ"ט:** הוא היה אומר (רבי עקיבא): האב זוכה לבן בנוי, ובכח, ובעושר, ובחכמה ובשנים ובמספר הדורות לפניו, והוא הקץ שנאמר: "קורא הדורות מראש" (ישעי' מא, ד).

3 **בראשית מז, כט:** ויקרבו ימי ישראל למות — פי' רש"י — כל מי שנאמרה בו קריבה למות, לא הגיע לימי אבותיו.

4 **בראשית מג, ב:** ויהי כאשר כלו לאכול — פי' רש"י — יהודה אמר להם, המתינו לזקן עד שתכלה פת מן הבית.

5 **רמב"ם הל' קריאת שמע פ"א ה"ד:** אמר להם, בני שמא יש בכם

פסלות? מי שאינו עומד עמי ביחוד השם כענין שאמר לנו משה רבנו, "פן יש בכם איש או אשה", וגו'"? ענו כולם ואמרו "שמע ישראל ה' אלקינו ה' אחד", כלומר: שמע ממנו אבינו ישראל, ה' אלקינו ה' אחד. פתח הזקן ואמר: ברוך שם כבוד, וכו'", לפיכך נהגו כל ישראל לומר שבח ששבח בו ישראל הזקן אחר פסוק זה.

6   **ב"ר ע, א**: ויד
ר ישראל — ישראל סבא.

7   **בראשית מח, ה**: ועתה שני בניך הנולדים לך בארץ מצרים עד באי אליך מצרימה לי הם. אפרים ומנשה כראובן ושמעון יהיו לי. פי' רש"י — בחשבון שאר בני הם, ליטול חלק בארץ איש כנגדו.

8   **שם מח, טז**: המלאך הגואל אותי מכל רע, יברך את הנערים ויקרא בהם שמי ושם אבותי, אברהם ויצחק וידגו לרוב בקרב הארץ.

9   **יבמות סב, ב**: בני בנים הרי הם כבנים, לענין מצות פריה ורביה. ראה בראשית מב, לח — "לא ירד בני עמכם", פי' רש"י — לא קבל דבריו של ראובן. אמר, בכור שוטה הוא זה, הוא אומר להמית בניו, וכי בניו הם ולא בני?

10   **רש"י, בראשית מח, א**: אפרים היה רגיל לפני יעקב בתלמוד. תנחומא ויחי — ,ויאמר מי אלה" — וכי לה היה מכירן? והלא בכל יום ויום יושבים ועוסקים בתורה לפניו, ועכשיו הוא אומר: "מי אלה"? לאחר ששמשו אותו י"ז שנה שעמד במצרים לא הכירן?

11   **מלאכי ג, כג-כד**: הנה אנכי שולח לכם את אלי' הנביא לפני בא יום ה' הגדול והנורא, והשיב לב אבות על בנים ולב בנים על אבותם.

CHAPTER II

THE SYMBOLISM OF BLUE AND WHITE

Introductory

The Torah prescribes: "Speak to the children of Israel and instruct them to make fringes, *tzitzit*, in the corners of their garments throughout the ages, putting a blue thread, *tekhelet*, in the fringes of each corner" (Num. 15:37).[1] The *tzitzit* remind us of our relationship with God, so that when "you look upon it, you will remember to do all the commandments of the Lord and will not follow your heart and eyes which lead you astray" (v. 39). The Talmud elaborates: "Looking [at the *tekhelet*] causes remembrance [of *mitzvot*]; remembrance causes doing" (Men. 43b).[2] Rashi explains how the heart and eyes engender temptation: "the heart and eyes are scouts for the body and act as its agents for sinning; the eye sees, the heart covets, and the body performs the transgression" (Num. 15:39).[3]

The *tzitzit* are a protective insignia, an identifying badge which is an antidote to forgetfulness. "There is no better reminder than to carry His seal on the garments one wears constantly, and one's eyes and thoughts are aware of it all the time, because the numerical value of the word *tzitzit* is 600, which together with the eight threads and five knots constitutes 613 (which is the number of commandments in the Torah) (Sefer Haḥinukh 386).[3a]

The Tur writes that "it is similar to one who attaches a string to the garment of another so that he should remember him." (Hil.Tzitzit 24)[4]

In addition, the color *tekhelet* directs our thoughts to the heavens, which are symbolically the color of God's Throne of Glory, namely, sapphire blue. The Talmud asks (Men. 43b): "Why was purple-blue, *tekhelet,* selected [for the fringes] rather than any other color? Because *tekhelet* resembles the [color of the] ocean, and the ocean resembles the sky, and the sky resembles the Divine throne" (see Ex. 24:10 and Ezra 1:26).[5] The *tekhelet* will, thereby, remind us of He who sits on the Throne of Glory (Rashi).

Like the *tefillin* on the arm opposite the heart, and the *tefillin* on the head over the seat of the intellect, and the *mezuzah* upon the doorposts of the home, so do the *tzitzit* instill in us an ever-awareness of God's providential closeness and deter us from sin (ibid.).[6]

Four Controversies

1. *Must We Have Both Blue and White?*

Must both colors, as mentioned in the Torah, be on the four-cornered garment in order to fulfill the *mitzvah?* What if all the threads are either white or blue? Our Sages discussed the matter: "The [absence of the] blue does not invalidate the white; the [absence of the] white does not invalidate the blue" (Men. 38a).[7] Though it is preferred to have both colors, the absence of either does not invalidate the *mitzvah.* This opinion of the Sages were disputed by R. Yehudah (Hanasi), who felt that both colors are required.

The accepted halakhah is in accordance with the majority view of the Sages that the fringes are acceptable with one color (Maimon., Hil. Tzitzit 1:4–5).[8] Had R. Yehudah's opinion prevailed, we would be unable to observe the *mitzvah* of *tzitzit* today because of the unavailability of the precise dye for *tekhelet.* Even in the days of the Mishnah, it had become exceedingly scarce.

2. *What Color is Tekhelet?*

Both Maimonides and Rashi agree that *tekhelet* is the color of the sky, *rakiah,* as the Talmud says clearly (Men. 43b),[5] but is it the daytime azure sky or the nighttime sky, which is navy blue or black? Both hues are equally inspirational in moving the psalmist to religious wonderment and ecstasy. "The heavens declare the glory of the Lord, and the expanse of the sky shows His handiwork; day following day [the rising and setting sun] brings expressions of praise, and night following night [the moon and the stars] reveals [His] wisdom" (Ps. 19:2–3).[9]

Maimonides was of the opinion that *tekhelet* is the color of the midday firmament seen in a cloudless sky, namely, azure (sky blue) (Hil. Tzitzit 2:1).[10] This color is suggested by the Talmud, which symbolically related the color of *tekhelet* to the Throne of Glory and to sapphire blue.[5] Thereby, *tekhelet* reminds us of Him who occupies the Throne.

Rashi, however, wrote that *tekhelet* resembles the sky when it darkens, *hamashhir l'et erev* (Num. 15:41),[11] close to sunset or after nightfall (navy blue or black). He relates the color to the tenth plague, *makat behorot,* which was inflicted upon the Egyptians at the time of the exodus of the Israelites. The word *tekhelet* resembles the Aramaic word *tikhla,* which means "bereavement," referring to the mass deaths of the tenth plague, which took place at night when the sky was dark. *Tekhelet,* according to Rashi, "resembles the sky when it darkens at eventide."

How are *tekhelet* and *tzitzit* related to the exodus? When the Israelites resided in Egypt, they wore an insignia which designated their vassal status. The Talmud called it *kavla d'avda,* which Rashi explains is "a seal worn by a slave on his garment to identify him as a slave" (Shab. 57b).[12] Upon achieving their freedom on the night of the exodus, they defiantly removed these seals. In exchange, they were to wear a new seal, *tzitzit* with *tekhelet,* indicating that henceforth they were to serve God, their new Master. "For unto Me the children of Israel are slaves; they are My slaves [they are to serve Me], whom I brought forth from the land of Egypt. I am the Lord your God" (Lev. 25:55).[13] Our Sages added: " 'unto Me they are slaves,' no longer are they slaves to their fellow man" (B. Kam. 116b).

This explains the inclusion of the verse referring to the exodus, *Yetziat Mitzrayim,* in the chapter which deals with the *mitzvah* of *tzitzit* (Num. 15:41).

The Or Haḥayyim (1696–1743) states this explicitly: "The *tzitzit* testify that the Israelites are God's slaves. When you look upon them, you will remember all the Lord's commandments. You will become aware that you are not free to do whatever you wish, but in all matters to act as a slave who is aware of his Master's authority."[14] In leaving Egypt, the Jews exchanged a human master for a Divine Master, an oppressive, exploitive, and degrading service for a morally exalting and spiritually privileged service of the Lord. The Egyptian *kavla d'avda* was replaced by *tzitzit.*

The Zohar offers a mystical interpretation of the color of the *tzitzit.* "*Tekhelet* suggests *Din,* the Divine attribute of strict justice; the white fringes suggest *Raḥamim,* the Divine attribute of compassion."[15] Even as the *tzitzit* alert us to our *mitzvah* obligations, we are informed that our failures will be judged by the attribute of *Din,* strict accountability (*tekhelet*) but tempered by an abundance of *Raḥamim* (white). This interpretation would accord with Rashi's view that *tekhelet* was dark blue or black and is reminiscent of the punitive judgment of *makat beḥorot* (the tenth plague). Maimonides' *tekhelet,* however, is clear and unthreatening and, together with the white threads, suggests the attributes of compassion and forgiveness.

3. *Ratio of Blue and White Threads.*

The fringes which are appended to each of the corners consist of four long threads drawn through a small hole about an inch from the corner and folded, thus comprising eight threads. According to Maimonides, one of the eight threads (one-half of one long thread) is colored *tekhelet* and seven are white. Ravad (1125–1198), noted for his strictures on Maimonides' Code of Law (Mishneh Torah), insists on a ratio of 2 to 6, namely, one long thread that is entirely *tekhelet.* Rashi and Tosafot prescribe a ratio of 4 to 4. The varying opinions support themselves on their interpretation of the Biblical text.[16]

4. Is There a Prescribed Dye?

The Talmud informs us that the dye for *tekhelet* was derived from a species of fish, *ḥilazon* (Men. 44), which was indigenous to the Mediterranean coastal area between Haifa and Tyre (or in the Dead Sea). Many assume that *ḥilazon* is the sole religiously authorized source for this dye. Maimonides ruled that the only requisite for *tekhelet* of *tzitzit* was that its lustrous beauty be durable and unchanging.[17] *Ḥilazon*, which was widely available in olden days, was the dye of first choice, but it was not mandated as the sole source of coloration, as though it had been legislated by Moses at Sinai.

Our Sages vehemently prohibited the substitution of a readily available vegetable dye caled *kalla illan* (indigo), though its appearance was identical to the *ḥilazon* dye, because its color faded with time. To counter deceivers, our Sages taught that "God will punish those who affix a thread of blue dyed with *kalla illan* and claim that it is really *tekhelet* [for *tzitzit*] (B. Metz. 61b).[18] *Ḥilazon*, therefore, is a metaphor for a perpetually blue dye. If another source of coloration were to be discovered or synthetically manufactured which would possess the required characteristics of lustrous durability, it would be halakhically acceptable for the *tekhelet of tzitzit*. (In actual fact, however, such has not been found and we follow the decision of the Geonim in their suspension of the requirement of *tekhelet*).[19]

Symbolism of Blue and White

Symbolically, the color white denotes clarity, distinctness, rationality, that which is self-evident. The prophet, referring to the power of *teshuvah* and God's forgiveness, speaks of white as synonymous with purity: "Though your sins be as scarlet, they shall be white as snow; though they be red as crimson, they shall become like fleece" (Isa. 1:18).[20] In modern Hebrew, the expression *hadevorim melubanim* (lit., the subject is white) means "the subject is crystal clear." In Talmudic usage, the Aramaic for "white" is *ḥavar* or *meḥuvar*, which means "is clear" or "it is proven."[21]

In the verse in Deuteronomy 22:17, referring to charges directed against a bride, the text says: "And they shall spread out the sheet before the elders of the town." Rashi explains: "This is a figurative expression. [It means that] they must make the matter 'as white as a sheet' [*meḥavrin hadevarim kesimlah*]." This is achieved by both parties bringing witnesses to clarify the facts of the case (Ket. 46a).[22] White, therefore, connotes clarity and certitude of judgment.

Tekhelet, in contrast, is the "likeness of the seas and the heavens,"[5] and focuses our thoughts on the grand mysteries of human experience which elude our precise understanding. The seas and heavens are boundless and beyond human reach. They encompass the abstract and the transcendent, ultimate values and ends, man's metaphysical quest and his efforts to rise above the self-evident and the temporal. It is this area which remains a perennial enigma, resisting rationalization and quantification. It is the realm of philosophy and religion which postulates truisms even as the great mystery persists and precise decipherment proves elusive. While the color white bespeaks the clearly perceptible, *tekhelet* refers to a realm which is only vaguely grasped.

In the Scientific Realm

All aspects of man's experience partake of blue and white. In the scientific inquiry, the physical sciences, i.e., physics, chemistry, biology, etc., lend themselves to mathematical precision; the universe is not erratic or capricious. Our ability to land men on the moon at a predetermined spot suggests a universe attuned to man's intellect. It is when the focus of inquiry changes to man's psyche and abstract verities that inexactitude and uncertainty intrude. Here one must labor with intuitive perceptions and be content with imprecise symbolic formulations. The social sciences, i.e., psychology, sociology, etc., therefore, are hampered by the indistinctness of their subject matter.

The ratio of white and blue threads, as taught by Maimonides, is illuminating in this context. The many threads of white, according to Maimonides, urge us to use our minds for discoveries in technology, to explore and master nature. The universe will yield its secrets to the organized scientific pursuit. But the one thread of *tekhelet* pertains to the spiritual realm, where man is humbled by the mystery of existence. Here he needs the guidance of revelation and the religious perceptions of the soul.

In Our Personal Lives

The same dichotomy between being on terra firma and on shifting sand is also experienced in our personal lives. We have all had periods, even of an extended nature, which are rational, planned, and predictable, when we feel that we have a hold on events. At other times, however, mystery and puzzlement intervene, dislocating the pattern of our lives and frustrating all our planning. No one can say, "The world and I have always gotten together reasonably, happily, and successfully, with ambitions always being realized. I have never been defeated." Stark and harsh reality often imposes the bizarre and the irrational, leaving us stupefied, shocked, and bereft. Inexplicable events render us humbled. This is the *tekhelet* of human experience.

The Enigma of Jewish History

If Jewish history operated solely with *lavan* (white), we would not be fighting for Israel today. From the standpoint of reason and logistics, our efforts against imponderable odds are insane. Building a homeland in a hotbed of hatred, surrounded by wealthy Arabs in enormous numbers whose opposition to Jewish strivings is seething and unabated, lacks all rational justification. Yet we struggle because the land was promised to us four thousand years ago. Gentiles, and even some assimilated Jews, view our dilemma from the vantage point of reasoned feasibility, and they cannot understand our obsession. Senator Humphrey, who was sympathetic to Israel, once said to Menachem Begin, "Please speak the language we understand, and not in riddles, symbols, or mysticism. Speak of politics and economics." We are astounded that Gentiles do not understand us; we want them to have a *tekhelet* approach, as we do, and to see Israel as interwoven with our religious consciousness. But only the Jew has his *tekhelet* perception.

Interpretation of the Four Controversies

Rabbi Judah (Rebbe) insisted that *m'akvim zeh et zeh,* that white alone—reasoned practicality—cannot sustain the Jew in history. Only with the *tekhelet* as well—his perception of God's involvement in history—can the Jew be motivated to persevere in face of all the travail and trauma inflicted by a hate-filled world. The Sages (*haḥamim*), however, ruled otherwise, teaching us that there are moments when *tekhelet* is lacking temporarily, when God seems inaccessible and events inexplicable—a situation which the Torah calls *hester panim*—and yet the Jew is expected to go on with his religious life and sacrifices. It almost seems as though God has abandoned His active surveillance over events, "as though I do not see their distress" (Rashi, Deut. 31:17).[23] Hopefully, this condition will be temporary, for, ideally, the Jewish garment should and will have both white and *tekhelet*.

The *tekhelet* of Jewish historical experience—His hovering presence—may, at times, be the color of Maimonides' midday blue, reflecting His benign *middat haraḥamim,* the warm glow of His lovingkindness, or the *tekhelet* may temporarily be dark, as Rashi taught, betokening the exacting relationship of *middat hadin,* the attribute of strict justice, when we only receive our due. *Tekhelet* may fluctuate in a ratio of only one thread or four, varying at different times and occasions. The Jew maintains his momentum and continuity of identity and religious loyalty under conditions which vary from the total absence of *tekhelet* to the presence of four threads of blue.

But on one quality all agree, that the *tekhelet* must possess a steadfast constancy of attractiveness. The commitment to *tekhelet* must be absolute, unwavering, because an intermittent loyalty would have rendered our people extinct centuries ago. No *kalla illan*—vegetable substitutes—will do which sparkle appealingly for a moment but then fade and succumb to adverse environmental conditions. Such presumptions of *tekhelet* are deceptive and bear no resemblance to genuine *tekhelet* which was initiated by our father Abraham at the dawn of our history. "For I have singled him [Abraham] out so that he may instruct his children and his posterity to keep the way of the Lord by doing what is just and right" (Gen. 18:19).[24] Historical durability is the test of authenticity.

Only a people sustained by *tekhelet* could be motivated to reconstitute a state after two thousand years of exile. Nations governed only by *lavan* (white) mock us incredulously and derisively. We are sustained by *tekhelet,* even when it is only a vision and temporarily obscured. The garment of Jewish life will yet possess both blue and white, and our historical yearnings and sacrifices will be vindicated.

הערות לפרק 2

1 **במדבר טו, לז**: ויאמר ה' אל משה לאמר: דבר אל בני ישראל ואמרת אלהם, ועשו להם ציצית על כנפי בגדיהם לדורותם, ונתנו על ציצית הכנף פתיל תכלת, והיה לכם לציצית וראיתם אותו וזכרתם את כל מצות ה' ועשיתם אותם, ולא תתורו אחרי לבבכם ואחרי עיניכם אשר אתם זונים אחריהם.

2 **מנחות מג, ב**: ראיה מביאה לידי זכירה. זכירה מביאה לידי עשיה.

3 **רש"י, במדבר טו, לט**: הלב והעינים הם מרגלים לגוף; מסרסרים לו את העבירות; העין רואה והלב חומד והגוף עושה את העבירה (תנחומא).

3a **ס' החנוך שפו**: ואין דבר בעולם יותר טוב לזכרון, כמו נשא חותם אדוניו קבוע בכסותו, אשר יכסה בו תמיד, ועיניו ולבו עליו כל היום ... כי מלת ציצית תרמוז לתרי"ג מצות עם צרוף שמונה חוטים שבציצית וחמשה קשרין שבו.

4 **טור, הל' ציצית סי' כ"ד**: דוגמא לדבר, כאדם המזהיר לחבירו על ענין אחד, שקושר קשר באזורו כדי שיזכירנו.

5 **מנחות מג, ב**: תניא, היה רבי מאיר אומר: מה נשתנה תכלת מכל מיני

צבעונין? מפני שהתכלת דומה לים וים דומה לרקיע לכסא
הכבוד, שנאמר "ותחת רגליו כמעשה לבנת הספיר וכעצם השמים
לטהר (שמות כד, י), וכתיב "כמראה אבן ספיר דמות כסא, פי' רש"י —
ומתוך התכלת מזכיר היושב על הכסא, ועוד, נאה לישראל שיהא
דמות כסאו עליהם.

6 **שם**: רבי אליעזר בן יעקב אומר: כל שיש לו תפילין בראשו ותפילין
בזרועו וציצית בבגדו ומזוזה בפתחו, הכל בחיזוק שלא יחטא שנאמר:
"והחוט המשולש לא במהרה ינתק" (קהלת ד, יב), ואומר, "חונה מלאך
ה' מסביב ליראיו ויחלצם" (תהלים לד, ח) — פי' רש"י, "ליראיו" —
העושים מצות. "ויחלצם" — את הצדיקים מחטא.

7 **מנחות לח, א (במשנה)**: התכלת אינה מעכבת את הלבן והלבן אינו
מעכב את התכלת; גמ' לימא מתניתין דלא כרבי, דתניא, וראיתם
אותו — מלמד שמעכבין זה את זה, דברי רבי, וחכמים אומרים אין
מעכבין.

8 **רמב"ם, הל' ציצית פ"א ה"ד-ה**: והתכלת אינו מעכב את הלבן והלבן
אינו מעכב את התכלת. כיצד? הרי שאין לו תכלת, עושה לבן לבדו
... אע"פ שאין אחד מהן מעכב את חברו, אינו שתי מצות אלא מצות
עשה אחת.

9 **תהלים יט, ב-ג**: השמים מספרים כבוד אל, ומעשה ידיו מגיד הרקיע,
יום ליום יביע אומר, ולילה ללילה יחוה דעת.

10 **רמב"ם, הל' ציצית פ"ב ה"א**: תכלת האמורה בתורה בכל מקום היא
הצמר הצבוע כפתוך שבכחול. וזו היא דמות הרקיע הנראית לעין
השמש בטהרו של רקיע. פי' כסף משנה: כתב כן דתניא בפרק התכלת,
"מה נשתנה תכלת מכל הצבעונין? מפני שהתכלת דומה לים וים
דומה לרקיע ורקיע לכסא הכבוד, וכו'".

11 **רש"י, במדבר טו, מא**: פתיל תכלת — על שם שכול בכורות, תרגומו
של "שכול" "תכלא": ומכתם היתה בלילה, וכן צבע התכלת דומה
לרקיע המשחיר לעת ערב; ושמונה חוטים שבה כנגד שמונה ימים
ששהו ישראל משיצאו ממצרים עד שאמרו שירה על הים. (ראה רש"י,
מנחות מג, ב — ד"ה דומה לים — שנעשו בו נסים לישראל).

12 **שבת נז, ב**: פי' רש"י ד"ה "אי כבבלא דעבדא תנן" — חותם שעושין
לעבד בכסותו לסימן הוכחה שהוא עבד; רש"י, מנחות מג, ב ד"ה
חותם — היו עושין לבהמה ולעבד כשקונין אותן לשם סימן עבדות.

13 **ב"ק קטז, ב**: כי לי בני ישראל עבדים, עבדי הם אשר הוצאתי אותם
מארץ מצרים, אני ה' אלקיכם (ויקרא כה, נה). אמר רב, פועל יכול
לחזור בו אפילו בחצי היום, שנאמר "כי לי בני ישראל עבדים ולא
עבדים לעבדים".

14 **אור החיים, במדבר טו, לט**: והציצית מעיד על ישראל שהם עבדי ה'
כדאיתא במס' שבת, כבלא דעבדא ... ואמר וראיתם אותו וזכרתם

את כל מצות ה', פי' כשיביטו בסימן עבדותם יתנו לב שאינם בני חורין לעשות כחפצם במאכלם, במלבושם, בדיבורם ובכל מעשיהם כעבד שאימת רבו עליו.

15 **זהר, שלח קעה**: מצות ציצית כליל תכלת ולבן, דינא ורחמי'.

16 **רמב"ם הל' ציצית פ"א ה"ו**: ומכניס שם ארבעה חוטים וכופלן באמצע ויהיה אחד משמונה החוטים חוט תכלת והשבעה לבנים. . .
פי' כסף משנה: וטעמו רבינו מדרכתיב "פתיל תכלת", פתיל חד משמע וכך כתב לחכמי לוניל והכי משמע בספרי: השגת הראב"ד — טעות הוא זה אלא השנים של תכלת והששה לבנים; רש"י — מנחות לח, א דמצוה לתת תכלת ב' חוטין ולבן שני חוטין בציצית; תוס' שם ד"ה התכלת אינה מעכבת את הלבן".

17 **רמב"ם שם פ"ב ה"א**: והתכלת האמורה בציצית צריך שתהיה צביעתה צביעה ידועה שעומדת ביופיה ולא תשתנה וכל שלא נצבע באותה צביעה פסול לציצית אע"פ שהוא בעין הרקיע.

18 **ב"מ סא, א**: שעתיד ליפרע ממי שתולה קלא אילן בבגדו ואומר תכלת היא: פי' רש"י קלא אילן צבע הדומה לתכלת (ראה רש"י במדבר טו, מא, שמפרש סמיכות "אני ה' אלקיכם").

19 **תפארת ישראל בקונטרוס "כללי בגדי קדש של כהונה" שבריש סדר מועד**: ז"ל: אמנם הדבר שאני מסופק בו, הוא אם באמת צריך לתכלת חלזון דוקא, דהנה כפי הנראה מהרמב"ם (כלי קדש פ"ח) שבתכלת שבבגדי כהונה א"צ חלזון . . . וכיון שהוכחנו שלתכלת שצריך לבגדי כהונה לא היה צריך חלזון דוקא, א"כ הוא הדין לגבי ציצית אין צריך לחלזון דוקא, דבשניהם לא נזכר רק מלת תכלת (ומביא עוד ראיה מירושלמי, פ' כלל גדול . . . רק דאפ"ה, אין נוהגין בתכלת בציצית מדאין אנו בקיאין באותן סממנים שהזכיר הש"ס שיבדקו בהם אם אינו משתנה כשיבדקוהו בהן.

21 **ישעי' א, יח**: אם יהיו חטאיכם כשנים, כשלג ילבינו. אם יאדימו כתולע כצמר יהיו.

22 **ב"ר צח, יד**: שהוא מחוור להם דברי תורה . . . שהוא מחוור להם טעותיהם.

דברים כב, יז: ופרשו השמלה לפני זקני העיר — פי' רש"י, הרי זה משל. מחוורין הדברים כשלמה; כתובות מו, א "מלמד שבאים עדים של זה ועדים של זה ובוררין את הדבר בשמלה חדשה".

23 **דברים לא, יז**: והסתרתי פני מהם — פי' רש"י, כמו שאיני רואה בצרתם.

24 **בראשית יח, יט**: כי ידעתיו למען אשר יצוה את בניו ואת ביתו אחריו ושמרו דרך ה' לעשות צדקה ומשפט.

The following two chapters are summarized adaptations of the Rav's classic essay, "The Lonely Man of Faith," *Tradition,* Spring 1965, pp. 5–67. While we have incorporated portions of the Rav's phraseology into our text, there is no substitute for an actual reading of the Rav's brilliant essay in its original, which is couched in his inimitable literary style.

CHAPTER III
THE MAN OF FAITH IN A TECHNOLOGICAL WORLD
Part I

The Basic Thesis

The history of man is a struggle of two Adams. One Adam sees his humanity realized in conquering the world, in the scientific harnessing of nature to man's service. This creative pursuit lends dignity to man and constitutes his uniqueness in the cosmos. The second Adam sees his human distinctiveness expressed in a worshipful relationship with God together with others in a faith-community. It is our thesis that it is the Jewish mandate to combine both proclivities. The Halakhah operates in the practical realm of reality, and an insular withdrawal from the creative act in the pragmatic world is contrary to the spirit of the Torah. Indeed, God wants man to function in both realms, despite his inevitable tensions and sense of uprootedness. This is his duty and destiny.

A Lonely Experience

Being people of faith in our contemporary world is a lonely experience. We live by doctrines which cannot be tested in the laboratory and are loyal to visionary expectations of a future which finds little support in present-day reality.

Our modern world is practical-minded. It reaches with confidence for distant galaxies, scoring ever-accelerating scientific breakthroughs and seeing in the here-and-now world of the senses the totality of human experience. Practical man lives in a technological world which is explained mathematically. Having victory after victory in his probing pursuits, modern man is confident, self-centered, and self-loving.

What can the man of faith, who is moved by sensitive reasons of the heart, say to a society which is governed by pragmatic reasons of the mind? It is not unusual for adherents of a particular faith to feel lonely if they are preponderantly surrounded by devotees of another creed. Abraham undoubtedly felt alone amidst his idol-worshipping neighbors. But the loneliness gripping the man of faith in the modern world is compounded, because he is confronted not only by competitive faiths, with their own forms of worship and transcendent claims, but by a pervasive and permissive culture which is ideologically secular and technologically successful. Religious faith is condescendingly regarded as a subjective palliative, but it is given little credence as a repository of truth.

We intend to define two types of man or, to be more precise, two tendencies of man—Adam I, whose creation is presented in the first chapter of Genesis, and Adam II, as portrayed in the second chapter. Adam I is technological man, whom we will call the "man of dignity," while Adam II is the "man of faith," and they both vie with each other for dominance. In our contemporary world, the man of dignity feels triumphant, while the man of faith feels besieged. We will delineate their different orientations and their points of confrontation, and show that in actuality there is only one Adam, seeking in alternating ways to assert his uniqueness in creation.

A clearer understanding of the dilemma faced by the man of faith may not solve his problems or relieve his solitude, but it will reassure him of his unique worthiness and of the objective value of his commitment. While loneliness can be discomfiting, to say the least, it can also be a source of invigoration, because feeling outwardly rejected presses one more deeply to the service of God. Though lonely and solitary, we are reassured that our service is wanted and gracefully accepted by God in His transcendent and luminous solitude. In any case, there is cathartic relief in talking, as Elihu the son of Barachel said: "I will speak so that I may find relief" (Job 32:21).[1]

Two Accounts of the Creation of Man

There are two accounts in early Genesis of the creation of man. We reject the theories of Bible critics who attribute these two accounts to different traditions and sources. Their hypotheses are misleadingly based on literary categories invented by modern man which are insensitive to the intellectual imagery of the Biblical story. We insist on the unity and integrity of Scripture and on its Divine character. The seeming incongruity of the two accounts, of which our Sages were aware,[2] speaks to us not of a dual tradition but of a typological duality in the nature of man. The two accounts deal with two types of Adam, two representatives of humanity, two fathers of mankind.

Text in Genesis I

"God [*Elohim*] created man in His image. In the image of God He created him; male and female He created them. God blessed them and said to them, 'Be fertile and multiply, and fill the land and subdue it [*v'khivshuha*]. Have dominion over the fish of the sea, over the birds of the sky, and over every beast that walks upon the earth' " (Gen. 1:27–28).[3]

Text in Genesis II

"The Eternal God [*Hashem Elohim*] formed man out of the dust of the ground and breathed into his nostrils a breath of life, and man [thus] became a living soul. The Eternal God planted a garden in Eden, to the east. There He placed the man that He had formed . . . to cultivate it and to watch it" (Gen. 2:7–8, 15).[4]

Textual Variations

There are four major discrepancies between these two accounts:

1. *Man's Formation.* Adam in Genesis I was created in the image of God, *b'tzelem Elohim,* but we are not informed how his body was formed. Adam in Genesis II was fashioned from the dust of the ground, with God breathing into him a breath of life.

2. *His Assignment.* Adam I received a mandate from the Almighty to fill the earth, subdue it, and have dominion over it, *milu et ha'aretz vekhivshuha, uredu.* Adam II was charged with the duty to cultivate the ground and to watch it, *le-avdah ul'shamrah.*

3. *Male and Female.* In the story of Adam I, both sexes were created concurrently, but Adam II emerged alone, with Eve appearing subsequently as his helpmate.

4. *Names of God.* In the first account, only the name *Elohim* appears, while in the second account *Elohim* is used in conjunction with the Tetragrammaton (*Hashem*).

Practical-Minded Adam I

Adam I is described as being in the "image of God," which Maimonides explains: "The characteristic endowment of a mentally normal human being is his intelligence. When the Torah says, 'let us make man in our image,' it refers to the human capacity to know and appreciate abstract conceptions, apart from particular physical objects" (Guide 1:1; Hil. Yesoday Hatorah 4:8).[5]

This superior intelligence equips man to be a creative being. Man's likeness to God expresses itself in his striving and ability to create, to confront the outside world, to inquire into its complex workings and interpret its varied components in their interrelationships. The Divine mandate "to subdue it [nature]" limits his intellectual attention to one quest, to harness and dominate the elemental forces and put them at his disposal. It is this practical interest which arouses his will to learn the secrets of nature. He is completely utilitarian. Adam I is not drawn to nature by any exploratory-cognitive curiosity. He is, rather, nurtured by a selfish desire to better his position in relation to his environment.

This practical pursuit of man's curiosity is clearly indicated by Naḥmanides' interpretation of the words "let them have dominion": "They shall rule vigorously over the fish, the birds, the cattle, and all creeping things. . . . They are to rule over the earth itself, to uproot and to pull down, to dig and to hew out copper and iron. The term *rediyah* [dominion] applies to the rule of a master over his servant" (1:26).[6]

Adam I is interested in just one aspect of reality and asks only one question: "How does the cosmos work?" He is not fascinated by the question "why does the cosmos function at all," nor is he interested in "what is its meaning or purpose." His sole motivation is to know how it works. He raises not metaphysical but only practical, technical questions.

Adam I Wants Dignity

Adam I wants to be a "man," to realize his humanity by being distinguishable from the rest of creation, by becoming the master over his environment. This grants him an honorable status with dignity. This is explicitly expressed in the words of the psalmist: "Thou hast made him a little lower than the angels and hast crowned him with glory and dignity. Thou hast made him to have dominion over the works of Thy hands. Thou hast put all things under his feet" (Ps. 8:6–7).[7] Dignity is equated by the psalmist with man's capability of dominating his environment and exercising control over it. Naḥmanides comments on this verse: "This refers to his intelligent, wise, and technically resourceful striving" (Gen. 1:26).[8]

Man attains dignity through his majestic posture vis-à-vis his environment. The brute's existence is not dignified, because it is a helpless existence. Man of old, who could not fight disease and succumed in multitudes to yellow fever or to other plagues, with degrading helplessness, could not lay claim to dignity. Only the man who builds hospitals, discovers therapeutic techniques, and saves lives is blessed with dignity. Man of the seventeenth and eighteenth centuries, who needed several days to travel from Boston to New York, was less dignified than modern man, who attempts to conquer space, who boards a plane at a New York airport and takes a leisurely walk several hours later in the streets of London. We are, of course, referring to Adam I as a type representing the collective technological genius and not to individual members of the human race.

Life in bondage to insensate elemental forces is an undignified affair. Animal life is helpless and, therefore, not dignified. Civilized man has gained limited control over nature and has become, in some respects, her master and, with his mastery, he has attained dignity. One further aspect inherent to his dignity must be emphasized. There is no dignity to Adam I's status without responsibility, as with a sovereign who presides over a realm. His freedom of action and creativity of mind are employed responsibly.

Creativity in Many Areas

Adam I is engaged in creative work, trying to imitate his Creator. The one in our modern world who most characteristically represents Adam I is the mathematical scientist, who creates a formal rational world woven out of numbers and their varied interrelationships. The mathematical world, such as was created by Einstein's creative imagination in the seclusion of his study, functions with amazing precision. The modern scientist does not try to explain nature, just to record its functioning.

As a creative agent of God, he constructs his own world and, in a mysterious fashion, succeeds in controlling his environment through his mathematical manipulations.

Adam I's creativity is not limited to the mind. He also creates beauty with his heart, in the physical and literary arts. He also creates legal systems to govern an orderly society. There can be no dignity in ugliness and political disarray. He is this-worldly minded; his conscience is energized not by the idea of the good (morality) or the true (intellectualism), but by the pleasant (aesthetic) and the functional (useful).

(It is interesting to note that Maimonides interpreted the story of Adam's sin in terms of betrayal of the intellectually true and the ethical for the aesthetically pleasant [Guide 1:2].)

Fulfilling God's Mandate

It is important to note that Adam I is not a rebel. He is merely carrying out God's mandate to him on the sixth day of creation, when God acknowledged his singularity by addressing him and summoning him to "fill the earth and subdue it." It is God who decreed that man shall not be a slave to his environment. Man, reaching for the stars, is acting in harmony with his nature, which was created, willed, and directed by his Maker. It is a manifestation of obedience to, rather than rebellion against, God. It was God who decreed that Adam I transform himself from man-slave to man-master, to venture into the open spaces of boundless exploration. Thus does man achieve dignity and majesty.

Faith-Minded Adam II

Adam the Second, like Adam the First, is also intrigued by the cosmos, to explain the *mysterium maqnum* of existence. While the cosmos provokes Adam I to seek power and control, Adam II responds to a different cognitive gesture. He does not ask functional questions which will help him to use the forces of nature. He does not ask "how" or "what" but "why," and "who."

He wonders: (a) Why was the world created, and why does nature seem indifferent and, at times, hostile to man's strivings? (b) From the depths of my being, I sense a message and challenge being directed at me. What is it? (c) Who is it who trails me steadily, like a persistent shadow, and vanishes into transcendence the instant I turn around and confront this numinous, awesome, and mysterious "He"? (d) Who is it to whom I cling in passionate all-consuming love, and of Whom I feel in mortal fear? Who is He whose life-giving and life-warming breath Adam II feels constantly, and who, at the same time, remains distant and remote?

To answer these questions, Adam II does not create a conceptual mathematical world, a useful method invented by Adam I. Adam II encounters the world directly, its color and grandeur, and bursts forth in ecstasy. "How manifold are Thy works, O Lord. In wisdom hast Thou made them all" (Ps. 104:24).

Adam II sees the world with the natural spontaneity of a child, who seeks the unusual and wonderful in every ordinary thing and event. While Adam I is dynamic and creative, using sense data to create concepts, Adam II reacts to the as is, not in mathematical formulae but in every beam of light and blossom. He seeks, not the abstract scientific world, but the intimate qualitative world. Not to be the master of nature, but to be in the service of its Creator, that is his primary aspiration.

Adam II experiences God intimately. This genuinely religious experience is symbolized by the Biblical metaphor, "He breathed into his nostrils the breath of life." While the "image of God" intelligence of Adam I refers to his intellectual endowment, the "breath of life" suggests an experiential closeness to God. Naḥmanides said: "It is stated that He breathed into his nostrils the breath of life because the soul was not formed from the [earthly] elements . . . nor did it emanate from the Separate Intelligence, but it was God's own breath" (Gen. 2:7).[9] The existential "I" has an awareness of this "Great Self" whose footprints he discovers along the many tortuous paths of creation.

What Motivates Adam II

Both Adams strive to be "human," to be what they inwardly perceive God wants them to be, namely, a human person. But their objectives and methodology differ, and their interpretive results inevitably are incommensurate. While Adam I declares his separateness and mastery over nature as the dignity and humanity he pursues, Adam II aspires, in addition, for the religious experience of sanctity, a sense of communion with the transcendent. An atheist cosmonaut, circling the earth, advising his superiors who placed him in orbit that he has not encountered any angels, might lay claim to dignity because he has courageously mastered space; he is, however, very far from experiencing holiness. He clearly typifies Adam I.

(continued in the next chapter)

הערות לפרק 3

1. **איוב לב, כ**: אדברה וירוח לי, אפתח שפתי ואענה.
2. ראה ברכות סא, א. כתובות ח, א. רמב"ן בראשית ב, ז. כוזרי פרק ד.
3. **בראשית א, כז-כח**: ויברא אלקים את האדם בצלמו, בצלם אלקים ברא אותו, זכר ונקבה ברא אותם. ויברך אותם אלקים ויאמר להם אלקים פרו ורבו ומלאו את הארץ וכבשוה ורדו בדגת הים ובעוף השמים ובכל חיה הרומשת על הארץ.
4. **שם ב, ז-ח, טו**: וייצר ה' אלקים את האדם עפר מן האדמה ויפח באפיו נשמת חיים ויהי האדם לנפש חיה, ויטע ה' אלקים גן בעדן מקדם וישם שם את האדם אשר יצר . . . ויקח ה' אלקים את האדם וינחהו בגן עדן לעבדה ולשמרה.
5. **מורה נבוכים א, א**: ובגלל ההשגה השכלית הזו נאמר בו "בצלם אלקים ברא אותו".
   הל' יסודי התורה פ"ד הל' ח: ועל צורה זו נאמר בתורה "נעשה אדם בצלמנו כדמותנו", כלומר, שתהא לו צורה היודעת ומשגת הדעות שאין להם גולם.

6 **רמב"ן, בראשית א, כו:** וטעם "וירדו", שימשלו בחזקה בדגים ובעוף ובבהמה ובכל הרמש, והבהמה תכלול החיה. ואמר "ובכל הארץ" שימשלו בארץ עצמה לעקור ולנתוץ ולחפור ולחצוב נחשת וברזל. ולשון "רדייה" ממשלת האדון בעבדו.

7 **תהלים ח, ו-ז:** ותחסרהו מעט מאלקים וכבוד והדר תעטרהו; תמשילהו במעשה ידיך כל שתה תחת רגליו.

8 **רמב"ן, בראשית א, כו:** כדכתיב "וכבוד והדר תעטרהו", והוא מגמת פניו בחכמה ובדעת וכשרון המעשה.

9 **רמב"ן, בראשית ב, ז:** ואמר כי הוא נפח באפיו נשמת חיים, להודיע כי לא באה בו מן היסודות (אש ורוח ומים וארץ)... גם לא בהשתלשלות מן השכלים הנבדלים (המלאכים) אבל היא רוח השם הגדול מפיו דעת ותבונה.

Chapter IV
THE MAN OF FAITH IN A TECHNOLOGICAL WORLD
Part II

Dignity is the goal of Adam I, which he majestically achieves through his domination of nature and by harnessing its power and resources to his service. Adam II does not seek to dominate nature but to serve that mysterious "He" he perceives in creation. In a word, Adam I seeks dignity and is practical-minded, while Adam II aspires for holiness and is faith-oriented. Both are responding to what they perceive as a Divine mandate to establish their singularity in the cosmos.

Adam I Needs a Work-Partner

Eve was created together with Adam I, "male and female He created them" (1:27).[1] He was not alone even on his first day of creation.

Why does Adam I need company? Being practical-minded, he needs help in responding to an often hostile and resistant environment. Helpless individuals realize that they cannot cope with life's multifarious needs and challenges when acting alone. Partnerships are formed, contracts are signed, and treaties of mutual assistance are made. Whenever the Adam I type of man wants to work, and creative activity is his primary interest, he must unite with others for practical reasons.

The verse in Genesis (2:18), "it is not good for man to be alone [lonely],"[2] is not applicable to Adam I, who is never lonely, because loneliness is nothing but the act of questioning one's legitimacy and worthiness. Adam I, in his majestic conquests, has no such self-doubts. He would change the verse into a utilitarian pronouncement, "It is not good for man to work alone." The words which follow, "I will make a compatible helper for him," *ayzer kenegdo,* would refer to a partner who collaborates and assists him in his undertakings. His simultaneous creation with Eve reflects his immediate need for a work partner to join him in nature's conquest and mastery.

Adam and Eve work together, yet each retains an "I" identity, not a "we" awareness. They communicate and satisfy each other's practical needs but are not bound to each other emotionally. Their inner-depth personalities do not connect. We all know relationships of this type, friendships or marriages, where a couple work and produce together but they do not coalesce; the relationship remains unhallowed. It is a surface association, in the pursuit of practical ends, not a soulful companionship, a fusion of identities. Such pragmatic relationships are best described by Ecclesiastes (Kohelet): "Two are better than one; because they have good reward for their labor. For if they fall, the one will lift up his fellow; but woe to him that is alone when he falleth and hath not another to lift him up" (4:9–10).[3]

Adam II Needs a Soul-Mate

While dignity is achieved through man's control of the environment, for which he needs a work-partner, sanctity for Adam II is acquired through Adam's control over himself. A hallowed life is a disciplined life which recognizes limitations. While Adam I surges forth without restraint, on the premise that whatever is possible is permissible, a sanctified Adam II confronts a Higher Will who commands him to retreat. Adam I was told to "fill the land and conquer it. Dominate the fish of the sea" (Gen. 1:28)[4] without limitation; Adam II was placed in the Garden of Eden "to cultivate it and to guard [preserve] it" (2:15).[5] While Adam I is proud and lordly in his self-estimation,

Adam II acknowledges his lowly origins, that he was "formed out of the dust of the ground" (2:7). He is a creature in privileged service of his Creator and is responsive to His every command. In what is essentially a religious gesture, Adam II circumscribes the range of his activities and indulgences in deference to the Divine, *va-yetzav,* "And He commanded."

Adam II profoundly feels his uniqueness, that he is alone with his sensitivities, that he is drastically different from the instinctual beasts whom he is commanded to name. "Whatever the man called each living thing remained its name" (Gen. 2:19). Naming is an act of critical classification which is based on a study of individual and group characteristics. He became aware that these life-forms do not partake of a hallowed existence. He must seek communion with intelligent, purposive beings like himself. The female who was created with Adam I would not satisfy him. She is a surface personality who, at best, can only be an associate, not a companion. It was, therefore, indispensable that Adam II, after experiencing unbearable solitude, contribute part of his being in the formation of a soul-mate, someone with whom he can communicate, a reflected counterpart of himself. With her he can form a faith-community, not merely a "work-community."

What is a faith-community? It is when three personae, "I," "thou," and "He" (God), are joined together in a covenantal commitment which is established through prophecy and prayer. Prophecy is when God talks to man, didactically as a teacher, prescribing through Revelation an ethico-moral code; prayer is man's worshipful response in commiting himself to these norms. Thus, a dialogue is achieved.

When man and woman participate in this tripartite covenant, they make a leap over the abyss separating two individuals. They are both charged with an ethico-moral mission, and in reaching out to God, they also reach to each other in sympathy and love, on the one hand, and in common action, on the other. While Adam I found Eve alongside him upon creation, Adam II was introduced to Eve by God; "And He [God] brought her to the man" (Gen. 2:22), and thus formed the first faith-community.

Adam and Eve, whose individual uniqueness is undecipherable to each other, in responding to God in prayer and commitment, overcame their loneliness with the help of the third party, God. In the faith-community, God's prophetic message demands a brotherliness between man and man, and the community of the committed becomes a commitment of friends. Thus are soul-partnerships achieved.

Elohim and the Tetragrammaton

God appears to Adam I in the first chapter of Genesis as *Elohim*, the Creator of the cosmos, of its power, natural laws, and mathematical equations. The word *Elohim,* from the Hebrew *el,* means "ruler of all natural forces" (Naḥmanides, Gen. 1:1).[6] A relationship with *Elohim* satisfies Adam I when, on occasion, he feels the need to acknowledge transcendence. His primary quest to master nature corresponds with his perception of the Divine Creator.

Adam II also sees *Elohim* in the panorama of nature and joins Adam I in proclaiming, "the heavens proclaim the glory of God [*El*], and the sky declares His handiwork" (Ps. 19:2).[7] (*El* is the abbreviated form of *Elohim*.) Yet, when he turns to Him in the splendor of nature, for solace and comaradeship, seeking a personal and intimate relationship with God, he finds Him remote. An affirmation of God derived from intellectual calculations, from studying the intricacy and grandeur of nature, is no substitute for an actual experience of His presence with the added elements of immediacy and certainty. Adam II seeks to apprehend God, not only to comprehend Him.

Abraham, the knight of faith, according to tradition, had searched for and discovered God in the sunlit heavens of Mesopotamia. From keen observation and philosophical analysis, he arrived at the conclusion of a unifying spiritual God and that all phenomena in the universe are the product of one directing intelligence.[8]

Yet, he felt an intense loneliness until he met God on earth as a Father and a Friend, when God spoke to him and foretold a great destiny for him and for his descendants. Abraham preached the practice of righteousness in imitation of an ethical, monotheistic God. In referring to his earlier life in his birthplace, Ur, Abraham said, "God, the Lord of heaven, took me away from my father's house and the land of my birth" (Gen. 24:7). The Midrash asks, why only "the God of heaven"? The explanation is that "until Abraham arrived, God reigned only over the heavens, but with Abraham, His sovereignty was extended to earth as well" (Sifri, 313, Ha'azinu).[9] It was Abraham who "crowned" Him God on earth, the God of men, making "His name a familiar one in people's mouths" (Rashi, Gen. 24:7; Ber. 59).

The communal encounter between God and man is expressed by the addition of the Tetragrammaton (Havayah) to *Elohim* in Genesis 2. God reveals Himself in the magnificence of the universe as *Elohim,* but what is more significant is that He is also manifest to him as a partner in the "faith-community." The name Havayah connotes an intimate experience of His presence, a communal closeness between God and man.

Combining Both Adams

We have been describing both Adams typologically, as though they were irreconcilable, separate persons with disparate temperaments and orientations. Actually, there is only one Adam with oscillating tendencies. The man of faith, in actuality, moves regularly between the faith-community and the work-community. He never remains totally immersed in the immediate awareness of being in God's presence. There is a continuous alternation between the cosmic and the covenantal, both areas being willed and sanctioned by God, who wants man to live creatively in this world even as he devoutly participates in the "faith-community."

This see-sawing between the cosmic and the covenantal is

reflected in the structure of the *berakhah* (blessing), in which we address God in both the second and third persons. We begin the *berakhah* with "Blessed art Thou," addressing God as "Thou," signifying that we are speaking to Him directly. Actually, it is this feeling that God has, indeed, revealed Himself to us in our immediate experience, in His goodness, or in a *mitzvah,* or in the wonders of nature, which prompts our blessing in the first place. But then, as we praise Him, we become aware that He is *Melekh ha-olam,* King of the entire universe, that His nature and rulership extend beyond our immediate experience. He is also manifest in the grandeur of His creation, and He bids us to engage in the creative majestic community as well. We therefore move from the second-person "Thou" to the third-person "who sanctified us with *His* commandments," *asher kidshanu b'mitzvotav.*

Initially we speak of "Thou" as we feel this closeness; we enlarge our concept to acknowledge Him as "King of the universe," and then we become overwhelmed by our presumption of intimacy with "Him" who is infinite, the highest majesty and the ultimate mystery, and we withdraw our address into a respectful third-person (Nahmanides Ex. 15:26).[10]

The Halakhah in the Practical World

The man of faith would prefer to remain withdrawn from the practical world and be engaged in day-and-night devotions. He will then find contentment in his comradeship with others of his faith-community. The Halakhah, however, commands him to leave the refuge of the faith-community and become involved in the worldly work community as a creative participant. Maimonides described the lives of the prophets, who were the ultimate men of faith, as follows: "When the prophetic communication ceased, all prophets [except Moses] returned to their daily practices and lived as others did and did not separate themselves from their wives" (Hil. Yesodei Hatorah 7:6).[11]

But even as he is engaged in worldly pursuits, the same

Halakhah does not let him forget that he is a covenantal being who will never find repose outside his God-awareness. He is commanded to abide by halakhic guidelines, "when you build a house" (Deut. 22:8), "when you cut your harvest" (ibid. 24:19), and "when you come into your neighbor's vineyard" (ibid. 23:25), and, at the same time, to "love the Lord with all your heart, with all your soul, and with all your might" (ibid. 6:5).[12]

There is not a single theoretical or technological discovery, from new psychological insights to man's attempts to reach out to the planets, with which the Halakhah is not concerned. New halakhic problems arise with every scientific discovery. In order to render precise halakhic decisions in many fields of human endeavor, one must possess, besides excellent halakhic training, a good working knowledge in those secular fields in which the problem occurs. This is clearly illustrated in the halakhic relationship to scientific medicine. The conquest of disease is a sacred duty; and on occasions of danger to human life, *piku'ah nefesh,* scientific medicine is regarded as authoritative in its diagnosis of the severity of the danger to life. In fact, most *mitzvot* address themselves to the pragmatic world where their performance takes place.

Adam I and Adam II are truly one person. In every one of us there abides the boldly creative and the devoutly submissive. Both tendencies are sanctioned by God. Rejection of either aspect of humanity is tantamount to a rejection of the Divine plan of creation, about which the Torah tells us, "And God saw all that He created and it was very good" (Gen. 1:31).

Dual Loneliness

If the man of faith remained exclusively in a cultural monastic retreat, his loneliness would be overcome by his closeness to God in fraternal devotion with others similarly committed. But in his involvement in the creative world, a sense of disquiet and uprootedness of spirit persists as he oscillates between two worlds. In the practical world, he lives a superficial existence;

in the covenantal world, he experiences religion in depth. He is consequently denied serenity of spirit and a sense of at-homeness in either world. This loneliness is discomfiting but inevitable.

In addition to existential loneliness, the man of faith is also subjected to social loneliness due to Adam I's condescension and his dismissal of the faith-community as superfluous and obsolete. Adam I denies that another Adam exists beside or, rather, in him. He is arrogant in his triumphs; his pride is boundless. He ignores the vital perceptions of Adam II and the significant contribution he could make to the contemporary world.

What Adam II Can Contribute

1. *Transcendental Depth.* Contemporary man is proud of his religious and cultural structures, which give dignity, pleasantness, and stability to his world. He attends lectures on religion and appreciates the ceremonial, yet he seeks, not faith, but a religious culture as a useful adjunct to life. It is not the divine but the social, not the covenantal but the aesthetic, which defines his religious devotions. Here, the man of faith can contribute depth and transcendental meaning by relating man to God in actual communion, by affirming Revelation and the objective reality of worship. There is more to religion than the pious gesture and the reassuring ceremonial.

2. *The Ethical Norm.* The ethical structure of the practical world cannot be upheld if not secured by God, the Higher Moral Will. Only the latter gives it fixity, permanence, and motivation. Rationalization and self-interest whittle away at man-derived ethics. Adam I's ethical standards are utilitarian and relativistic; they are not anchored in the absolute. The dire consequences are rampantly manifest in our modern world. Adam II would envelop ethics with Godliness and restrain man's rampaging nature.

3. *In Crisis.* Adam I feels triumphant and self-sufficient when

things go well. His world yields to his demand. In moments of insecurity and fright, however, he is hopelessly adrift and depressed. Only Adam II can pray, "Out of the depths, I call unto Thee, O Lord" (Ps. 130:1) or echo the words of Job, "The Lord gave, the Lord hath taken; praised be the name of the Lord" (Job 1:21).

Though he is often regarded as an irrelevance in the modern world, the man of faith keeps his rendezvous with eternity and persists tenaciously in bringing the message of faith to the majestic world. In this historical mission, the lonely man of faith meets the Lonely One who resides in the recesses of transcendental solitude. This is the sacrificial but privileged role of the man of faith.

הערות לפרק 4

1. **בראשית א, כז**: ויברא אלקים את האדם בצלמו, בצלם אלקים ברא אותו, זכר ונקבה ברא אותם.
2. **שם ב, יח**: ויאמר ה' אלקים: לא טוב היות האדם לבדו אעשה לו עזר כנגדו.
3. **קהלת ד, ט-י**: טובים השנים מן האחד, אשר יש להם שכר טוב בעמלם, כי אם יפלו האחד יקים את חברו, ואילו האחד שיפול, ואין שני להקימו.
4. **בראשית א, כח**: ויברך אותם אלקים ויאמר להם אלקים, פרו ורבו ומלאו את הארץ וכבשוה ורדו בדגת הים, ובעוף השמים ובכל חיה הרמשת על הארץ.
5. **שם ב, טו**: ויקח ה' אלקים את האדם וינחהו בגן עדן לעבדה ולשמרה.
6. **רמב"ן, בראשית א, א**: "ויאמר אלקים" בעל הכחות כולם, כי המלה עיקרה אל, שהוא כח, והיא מלה מורכבת אל הם (רצונו לאמר כי הכחות כולם הם מאת העליון יתברך ולכן נקרא אלקים אשר בו כח ואילות, כלומר, מאל הם) (הכתב והקבלה).
7. **תהלים יט, ב**: השמים מספרים כבוד א-ל, ומעשה ידיו מגיד הרקיע.
8. רמב"ם הל' ע"ז פ"א-ג: והיה תמה: האיך אפשר שיהיה הגלגל הזה נוהג תמיד ולא יהיה לו מנהיג? ומי יסבב אותו... עד שהשיג דרך האמת והבין קו הצדק מתבונתו הנכונה. וידע שיש שם אלוה אחד והוא מנהיג הגלגל, והוא ברא את הכל, ואין בכל הנמצא אלוה חוץ ממנו.

9 **בראשית כד, ז**: פרש"י "ה' אלקי השמים", ולא אמר "ואלקי הארץ", ולמעלה אמרינן "ואשביעך בה' אלקי השמים ואלקי הארץ"? אמר לו: עכשיו הוא אלקי השמים ואלקי הארץ, שהרגלתיו בפי הבריות, אבל כשלקחני מבית אבי, היה אלקי השמים ולא אלקי הארץ, שלא היו באי עולם מכירים בו ושמו לא היה רגיל בארץ.

10 ראה רמב"ן, שמות טו, כו.

11 **רמב"ם הל' יסודי התורה פ"ז ה"ו**: "שובו לכם לאהליכם ואתה פה עמוד עמדי" (דברים ה, כז-כח) הא למדת, שכל הנביאים (חוץ ממשה) כשהנבואה מסתלקת מהם, חוזרים לאהלם [לביתם ולחיי משפחתם כמקודם], שהוא צרכי הגוף, כולם כשאר העם, לפיכך אין פורשים מנשותיהם.

12 **דברים כב, ח**: כי תבנה בית חדש ועשית מעקה לגגיך. כי תבא בכרם רעך, ואכלת ענבים כנפשך שבעיך ואל כליך לא תתן (שם, כג, כה). כי תקצור קצירך בשדך, ושכחת עומר בשדה, לא תשוב לקחתו, לגר ליתום ולאלמנה יהיה (שם כד, יט).

CHAPTER V

AS A BRIDEGROOM WITH HIS BRIDE

The Jewish nuptial service consists of two parts, betrothal (*Erusin*) and marriage (*Nesuin*), each of which is performed over a cup of wine. The first part, called "Blessing of Betrothal" (*Birkhat Erusin*), establishes the legal bond between the parties. God is praised (thanked) for ordaining the laws of morality and, thereby, "sanctifying His people Israel through the institution of marriage."[1] Marriage, being of Divine origin, proscribes illicit relations and extols consecrated wedlock.

The second part, "Blessings of Marriage" (*Birkhot Nesuin* or *Ḥatanim*), celebrates the completed nuptial. In a series of seven blessings (*Sheva Berakhot*), various themes are highlighted: God is the Creator of the world, whose purpose is to be realized through man and woman, who were formed, spiritually, in God's image. As He gladdened the first human couple, Adam and Eve, in the Garden of Eden, "so may abundant joy embrace these loving companions" (bride and groom). May their unfolding personal happiness coincide with the anticipated Messianic rejoicing of the entire Jewish people, when "sounds of joy and gladness will soon be heard in the cities of Judah and the streets of Jerusalem."

Being mindful of Jerusalem and of its travails in moments of personal joy is in fulfillment of the oath our ancestors took on the shores of Babylon after the destruction of the Temple in 586 B.C.E. "If I forget thee Jerusalem, let my right hand lose its strength, let my tongue cleave to the top of my mouth, if I remember thee not, if I set not Jersualem above my chief joy." (PS. 137:5, 6)[2]

The first blessing of the *Sheva Berakhot* is over a cup of wine, because "wine gladdens the heart of man" (Ps. 104:15); the second blessing proclaims that there is a spiritual purpose to God's creation of the world, *she-hakol bara likhvodo*.

An Analysis of the Third and Fourth Blessings

The third and fourth blessings of the *Sheva Berakhot* read, respectively, "Blessed are You, O Lord our God, King of the universe, who formed man [*yotzer ha-adam*]," and "Blessed are You, O Lord our God, King of the universe, who formed man in His image, after His likeness, and made for him, for all time, a woman out of his very self. Blessed are You, O Lord, who formed man [*yotzer ha-adam*]."[3]

Both blessings acknowledge God's creation of man (*yotzer ha-adam*), and this apparent repetitiveness makes them deserving of analysis. Why have two blessings affirming the same theme, that God is man's creator?

Because of its brevity, the third blessing opens with "blessed are You" (*Barukh Atah*), but does not conclude with *Barukh Atah*, as longer blessings generally do.[4] Man's creation is pithily and gratefully acknowledged without further elaboration. It is structurally similar to *birkhot hanehenin*, such blessings as are recited prior to personal enjoyment of foods or the performance of *mitzvot*. The fourth blessing, however, has auxiliary themes, citing man's Divine image and Eve's formation "out of his very self," and concludes with *Barukh Atah*.

Since the fashioning of man is celebrated in the more elaborately formulated fourth blessing, why was there a need for the third blessing? Also, what do the additional themes of the fourth blessing tell us regarding man's nature and purpose which would be of interest to the bride and groom?

Man's Dual Nature

An analysis of the Biblical creation chapter indicates that man is composed of two components, each vying with the other for dominance. These two blessings of the *Sheva Berakhot*, far from being repetitive, allude to two distinct and often antithetical levels of human existence. The bride and groom are invited, as it were, to choose the grander and loftier commitment embodied in the more exacting fourth blessing.

The Torah records man's creation as follows: "The Lord God formed [*va-yitzer*] man from the dust of the ground, [*afar min ha-adamah*], and He breathed into his nostrils the breath [soul] of life, *va-yipaḥ b'apav nishmat ḥayyim*" (Gen. 2:7). Rashi adds: "[Here we have two *yud*s, in the word *va-yitzer*, to intimate] a double formation, one for this world [body], and the other, to attain the resurrection [of the righteous (soul)]. In the case of animals, which are not spiritually accountable, the word *va-yitzer* is not written with two *yud*s. . . . He made him of both earthly and heavenly matter, the body of the earthly and the soul of the heavenly."[5]

Man is a duality; he partakes of two identities. He is a natural being, *afar min ha-adamah*, subject to biological needs common to all animal life. He is a child of nature, a *homo natura*, studied by scientists as part of the zoological system. But man also possesses transcendental yearnings and is not content with mere self-preservation and physical indulgence. An intuitive sense informs him that he possesses a soul whose origin and destiny transcend his animal existence.[6] This metaphysical self-awareness of a qualitative uniqueness reflects the *nishmat ḥayyim* dimension which God breathed into him at creation. This is his Divine image.

Since man combines within himself such antithetical natures, we are at loss how to classify him. Modern anthropology and, indeed, most of the social sciences, reflecting a secular bias, place man in the Mammalian class, at the apex of evolutionary development. This is widely accepted, though it is obvious to objective observers and to man himself that he differs strikingly from animal life. His intellect, moral sense, creative capacity, and questing soul bespeak a superiority and singularity in all creation.

The Torah, even as it acknowledges man's physical nature and provides for its fulfillment, insists that man can exercise his free will to choose a higher and more sublime identity. In terms of physical strength and size, man may be inferior to some animals, but his spiritual identity, to which he can give primacy, elevates him to a status of "but little lower than the angels" (Ps. 8:6).

The Third Blessing

These two identities of man are inherent in the third and fourth blessings of the *Sheva Berakhot*. The shorter blessing is for man in the natural kingdom, as he is casually listed and impersonally designated in the first chapter of Genesis, as "male and female" *zakhar u'nekevah* (v. 7), instead of being identified as Adam and Eve. On that first Friday afternoon, man's formation followed other forms of life, beasts, cattle, and creeping things (v. 25) with whom he shared a similar biology. In fact, our Sages suggest that man was created last, following the other animals, in order to deflate his ego and to humble him in the realization that only his spiritual soul made him superior (Sanh. 38a).[7]

As such, this blessing reflects the animalistic nature of man, and it is, therefore, structurally similar to those we recite in gratitude to God for the produce of the earth, *birkhot hanehenin*, for man, too, is of the earth, *min ha-adamah*. For natural, mundane-minded man, this brief blessing is appropriate; nothing more need be added.

It is significant to note that even in Genesis 1, the Torah informs us that man was created in God's image (v. 27), suggesting that he has the potential to transcend his animal identity. His Divine image is not, at this point, a spiritual endowment already achieved, but a goal for him to attain. It is a potentiality to be realized. It is an exhortation, not a characterization; it calls upon him to live like a creature who bears a resemblance to his Maker.

The Fourth Blessing

Chapter 2 of Genesis introduces us to a higher category of man. This new dimension is found in the fourth blessing, which refers to man's Divine image, *b'tzelem demut tavnito*. He is a being who is individually worthy of being addressed by God. He is also capable of forming enduring relationships, as with Eve, *binyan adei ad*. He is truly unique, as taught by our Sages: "Why was man created as an individual? To teach us that he who destroys one life in Israel, it is as if he destroyed the entire world; and he who saves one life in Israel, it is as if he saved the entire world . . . each individual can thus claim that it is for me that the world was created" (Sanh. 37a).[8] We have here an affirmation of individual human worth.

Each individual possesses something unique which is unknown to others. Each individual has a special message to communicate, a particular color to add to the communal spectrum. He exists once in eternity. The halakhic rules pertaining to mourning, *avelut*, are rooted in this perception of the singleness of man. He is a universe unto himself; with the death of an individual, a little world comes to an end, a vacuum which others cannot fill. The fourth blessing is, therefore, longer than the third, a *berakhah arukhah*, metaphysically as well as literally, because broader themes are here denoted. Man is acknowledged as capable of higher levels of existence, and there is more to his identity than the mere fact of his creation by God.

Man's Individual Worth

How man is defined has profound implications regarding his place in society and his role in history. If man be but a sophisticated animal, he cannot legitimately claim for himself a greater dignity or worthiness than his fellow creatures. Maimonides taught: "In the lower and subluminary portion of the universe, Divine Providence [*hashgachah*, God's compassionate concern] does not extend to individual members of the species [of animals], except in case of mankind. It is only in this species [man] that what happens to individual beings, their good and evil fortune, is the result of justice, in accordance with the words 'for all His ways are judgment' [Deut. 32:4]" (Guide 3:17).[9]

Unlike man, who was created as a solitary being, animals and vegetation were formed "after their kind," *l'mino*, in aggregates and in substantial numbers. God's only concern is the preservation of the species, and no metaphysical worthiness or singularity attaches to individual creatures. They are expendable and easily replaceable. Man, however, is individually valued.

Secularists, who reject man's metaphysical pretensions, implicitly impair his claims of individual worthiness. Man can no longer claim "inalienable rights" as affirmed in the Magna Carta and the Declaration of Independence. These and other human rights documents lose their philosophical support. If the individual is significant only by virtue of his being part of the collective, *l'mino*, then man may be legitimately exploited and abused if it serves some presumed higher social good. Millions were slaughtered by Stalin and Hitler for presumed social ends. Man cannot claim individual rights as an autonomous being. This is statism, the total empowerment of the state at the cost of individual liberty. Ultimately, it is fascism and communism.

The secularization of man's status in the modern world by scholarly disciplines has, indeed, resulted in such dehumanization. The anthropological view of man denies him singularity and transcendental worthiness. If he is only *min ha-adamah*, then he is individually of little consequence, and such devaluation invites such horrors as our modern world has witnessed.

If, however, man possesses a spiritual dimension, then his individual worthiness is never lost. He has obligations to the community, but the latter is not an ultimate value. The state is subject to the will of its members, who control it and, in effect, determine its course and destiny. This is the philosophical foundation of the democratic ideal. Democracy and human rights are rooted in the premise of the uniqueness of individual man. Only an identity derived from *be-tzelem demut tavnito* can entrust such dignity to man.

Two Kinds of Marriage

The third and fourth blessings suggest different dimensions of marriage. The former, as in Genesis 1, speaks of man's creation along with other animal creatures where individual worth is subordinated to the primacy of the species. Accordingly, marriage is a biologically motivated and socially stabilizing institution, where personal happiness and mutual respect are incidental and irrelevant. Group interests and social respectability are primary. Such mating is functional, exploitive, and, at times, subversive of human dignity.

A profoundly loftier marriage is inherent in the fourth blessing, which notes the transcendental worthiness of two individuals, each endowed with a *tzelem demut tavnito*, each accountable to God. Each possesses the Divine "breath of life" and is inestimably worthy.

The ceremonies surrounding the wedding reflect a high regard for the happiness and fulfillment of the bride and groom. In the *Sheva Berakhot*, we pray that He who "rejoices the bridegroom and the bride," *mesamme'ah hatan v'kallah*, may bless their marriage with "love and harmony, peace and friendship," *ahavah, v'ahvah, v'shalom v're'ut*. The School of Hillel taught that in dancing before the bride, we should say, "O beautiful and kindly bride" (Ket. 16b).[10] The couple are regaled for seven days after their nuptial with feasts arranged by family and friends, *shivat yemei hamishteh*, during which the *Sheva Berakhot* are repeated (Ket. 8b).[11] So inviolable is the festivity of this period that it even postpones the onset of *shivah* (mourning) if either the bride or groom suffers the death of a close relative (Rambam, Hil. Avel 11:7).[12]

Social Responsibility

We have emphasized personal worth and individual fulfillment, which can be mistaken for an exclusive self-concern. Such a posture is morally reprehensible and violates the letter and spirit of the Torah. The verse "You shall love your neighbor as yourself" (Lev. 19:18), which Rabbi Akiba declared to be a cardinal precept of the Torah, *zeh klal gadol ha-Torah*, commands a caring concern for our fellow man. This social responsiveness is derived from one's healthy self-regard, namely, "as [you love] yourself." Individual importance is emphasized, but for goals beyond self-indulgence; personal fulfillment is valued, but for sublime purposes.

This may explain why the *Sheva Berakhot* relate the personal happiness of the groom and bride to the Messianic fulfillment. "Soon, O Lord our God, may there be heard in the cities of Judah and the streets of Jerusalem a sound of gladness, a sound of joy, the sound of the bridegroom and the sound of the bride, the sound of rejoicing bridegrooms at their weddings" (*meherah . . . yishama*; based on Jer. 33:10–11).[13] We find a similar correlation in Isaiah 62:5, "As the bridegroom rejoices over his bride, so shall God rejoice over thee [Zion]" (*yasis alayikh Elohayikh*).[14] The couple is challenged to reach out to *Knesset Yisrael*, to identify with the strivings of the broader community, its travails and its triumphs, and thereby to hasten the coming of the Messiah.

The Ideal Marriage

In his commentary on the Mishnah, Maimonides elaborates on the teaching, "Acquire a companion for yourself" (Av. 1:6), by describing three levels of friendship.[15]

1. *Pragmatic Friendships (ḥaver le-ezrah)*. This is a utilitarian association where two people need each other for practical benefits, as in a business partnership. When their mutual needs cease, their friendship lapses. There is no other bond between them (*batel davar, betelah ahavah*—Av. 5:19).

2. *Empathetic Friendships (ḥaver lid'agah)*. Such comradeship involves a caring responsiveness, a sharing of innermost feelings, both sad and joyful. Life's burdens are lightened and its celebrations are heightened in a relationship of emotional rapport which is rooted in faith and confidence. Such friendships are firmly based and enduring.

3. *Value Friendships* (*ḥaver l'de'ah*). This association allows for the deepest level of friendship to thrive, for besides their being committed to each other, they share a dedication to a noble ideal and value. They collaborate towards the furtherance of a lofty cause. Theirs is a unity of purpose and a joining of dreams. Their relationship is deepened and ennobled as they transcend their personal concerns.

A marriage which is strictly utilitarian, of mutual exploitation, cannot rise above the *min ha-adamah* level. It lacks human dignity and is inherently fragile. A meaningful marriage must, at the least, partake of the second level, which reflects a depth of feeling for each other. But it is only with the addition of the third level that a marriage assumes a sublimity of purpose. Two individuals are joined by a noble vision. This dimension of *nishmat ḥayyim* makes for an ideal marriage.

הערות לפרק 5

1 **כתובות ז, ב**: ברוך אה"ה ה', מקדש ישראל על ידי חופה וקידושין.
2 **תהלים קל"ז, ה-ו**: אם אשכחך ירושלים תשכח ימיני, תדבק לשוני לחכי, אם לא אזכרכי, אם לא אעלה את ירושלים על ראש שמחתי.
3 **כתובות ח, א**: בא"י, אמ"ה, יוצר האדם: בא"ש, אמ"ה אשר יצר את האדם בצלמו בצלם דמות תבניתו, והתקין לו ממנו בנין עדי עד, בא"י, יוצר האדם.
4 **ברכות יא, א**: אינו רשאי לחתום — פי' רש"י — כגון ברכת הפירות והמצות (כיון שאין בהם ענינים הרבה, פתיחתן הן חתימתן — תוס' רבי' עקביא איגר).
5 **בראשית ב, ז**: וייצר ה' אלקים את האדם עפר מן האדמה ויפח באפיו נשמת חיים — פי' רש"י — שתי יצירות, יצירה לעולם הזה ויצירה לתחיית המתים. אבל בבהמה שאינה עומדת לדין, לא נכתב ביצירתה שתי יודי"ן . . . עשאו מן התחתונים ומן העליונים, גוף מן התחתונים ונשמה מן העליונים.
6 **אבות ג, יח**: חביב אדם שנברא בצלם, חיבה יתירה נודעת לו שנברא בצלם שנאמר "כי בצלם אלקים עשה את האדם" (בראשית ט, ו).
7 **סנהדרין לח, א**: אדם נברא בערב שבת ומפני מה? שאם תזוח (תתגאה) דעתו עליו, אומר לו, יתוש קדמך במעשה בראשית.
8 **סנהדרין לז, א**: לפיכך נברא אדם יחידי, ללמדך שכל המאבד נפש

אחת מישראל מעלה עליו הכתוב כאילו איבד עולם מלא וכל המקיים נפש אחת מישראל מעלה עליו הכתוב כאילו קיים עולם מלא, לפיכך כל אחד ואחד חייב לומר בשבילי נברא העולם.

9 **רמב"ם, מורה נבוכים ח"ג פי"ז (תרגום קאפח)**: אני בדעה כי ההשגחה האלקית אינה בעולם הזה השפל, כלומר מתחת גלגל הירח אלא באישי (כל יחיד וכל פרט) מן האדם בלבד ... אבל שאר בעלי חיים וכ"ש הצומח וזולתו הרי השקפתו בו כהשקפת אריסטו (שההשגחה מחייב קיום המינים ותמידותם ולא יתכן קיום אישיהם) ואשר הביאני לדעה זו לפי שלא מצאתי כל לשון ספר נביא שמזכיר שיש לה' השגחה באיש מאישי בעלי חיים (בפרט מפרטי) זולתי באישי האדם לבד.

10 **כתובות טז, ב**: תנו רבנן כיצד מרקדין לפני הכלה? בית שמאי אומרים כלה כמות שהיא, ובית הלל אומרים כלה נאה וחסודה.

11 **כתובות ח, ב**: אמר רבי יצחק אמר רבי יוחנן: מברכים ברכת חתנים בעשרה כל שבעה וחתנים מן המנין.

12 **רמב"ם, הל' אבל פי"א ה"ז**: שבעת ימי החתונות הרי הן כרגל ומי שמת לו מת בתוך ימי המשתה אפילו אביו ואמו משלים שבעת ימי השמחה ואחר כך נוהג שבעת ימי אבלות ומונה השלשים מאחר ימי השמחה.

13 **כתובות ח, א**: מהרה ה' אלקינו ישמע בערי יהודה ובחוצות ירושלים, קול ששון וקול שמחה, קול חתן וקול כלה, קול מצהלות חתנים מחופתם ונערים ממשתה נגינתם.

14 **ישעי' סב, ה**: ומשוש חתן על כלה, ישיש עליך אלקיך.

15 **רמב"ם, פירוש למשניות**: וקנה לך חבר (אבות א, ו), והאוהבים שלשה מינים, אוהב תועלת, אוהב מנוחה ואוהב מעלה. (א) אוהב תועלת כאהבת שני שותפים. ב) אוהב מנוחה הוא שיהיה לאדם אוהב תבטח נפשו בו, לא ישמר ממנו במעשה ולא בדבור ויודיעהו כל ענייניו, הטוב מהם והמגונה מבלתי שירא ממנו שישיגהו בכל זה חסרון, ומצא מנוחה גדולה בדבריו ובאהבתו. (ג) ואוהב מעלה הוא שיהיה תאות שניהם וכונתם לדבר אחד והוא הטוב וירצה כל אחד להעזר בחבירו בהגיע הטוב, הוא לשניהם יחד, וזה האוהב אשר צוה לקנותו והוא כאהבת הרב לתלמיד והתלמיד לרב.

רמב"ם אבות ה, טז: ומפני זה כשתהיה סיבת האהבה ענין אלקי וה המדע האמיתי, האהבה ההיא אי אפשר שתסור לעולם מפני שסבו מחמדת המציאות.

CHAPTER VI

SHAPING JEWISH CHARACTER

The Two Covenants

We are members of an enigmatic covenantal community which was formed with our ancestor, Abraham. A covenant is a mutually established compact, an agreement binding one or several parties to particular obligations. Jewish history speaks of two primary covenants established by God with the Jewish people. The first was the Patriarchic Covenant, which was concluded with Abraham (Gen. 15:8, 17:1), repeated with Isaac (ibid. 26:2), and again with Jacob (ibid. 28:13–16). The second was the Sinaitic Covenant, the Revelation at Mount Sinai, *Mattan Torah,* in which the entire Jewish people, *Kenesset Yisrael,* participated (Ex. 19). This covenant was repeated by Moses in the plains of Moab (Deut. 29:9) before they entered Eretz Yisrael and again by Joshua (24:25) in Eretz Yisrael before his death.

The nature of the Sinaitic Covenant and its enduring meaning for all future generations is clear. The Jewish people individually and collectively committed itself and all future generations[1] to the observance of the Commandments, *taryag mitzvot,*[2] to which no other people was obligated. In Jewish Law, *Halakhah,* one who commits to writing a statement of monetary indebtedness, *shetar hithayvut,* and delivers the document, assumes a legal obligation to remit the indicated amount. Similarly, the Sinaitic Covenant precipitated on the part of the Jews an indebtedness to observe a distinctive regimen of commandments, and God, as the second party (or the first) of the contract, adopted them as His treasured people, *Am Segulah.* Indeed, the Tablets of the Law (Decalogue) are called *luḥot ha-edut* because they testify to the covenantal agreement (Rashi, Ex. 25:16).[3]

What is puzzling, however, is the Patriarchic Covenant, which does not seem to have imposed any particular commandments upon the patriarchs and upon future generations, except for circumcision which is an *ot,* an insignia of the covenant.[4] God, as the text indicates, did promise them the Holy Land as an historical inheritance (Gen. 15:18) and to maintain a singular relationship with them in history (17:7). But what did the covenant impose upon the Jewish people, and what has been its enduring relevance and influence over the centuries?

The Importance of the Patriarchic Covenant

The Patriarchic Covenant is frequently referred to in our Scriptures and by our Sages as the foundation upon which all of Jewish history is based. In Lev. 26:42–44 (*Toḥakhah*), the Torah informs us that when Israel will be direly punished for its sins, God will be stirred to mercy by recalling the covenant which He had concluded with their noble ancestors. "Then will I remember My covenant with Jacob, and also My covenant with Isaac, and also My covenant with Abraham will I remember; and I will remember the land."[5] Three verses later, the Torah adds that they will be spared total annihilation in remembrance of the Sinaitic Covenant.[6] But the Patriarchic Covenant comes first.

Similarly, in the Rosh Hashanah *Musaf* liturgy called *Zikhronot,* which is an affirmation that God remembers the deeds of men and of nations, both covenants are mentioned, with primary precedence being given to the Patriarchic Covenant, the *brit avot*. Wherein is the special significance of the Patriarchic Covenant? The primary potency of the Patriarchic Covenant was acknowledged in the Talmud: "When Israel sinned in the desert, Moses rose before the Lord and said many prayers and petitions without effect. When he added, 'Remember the covenant of Your servants Abraham, Isaac, and Jacob,' God immediately responded" (Shab. 30a).[7]

The Patriarchic Covenant apparently imparts teachings to the Jewish people by example rather than by prescription. While the Sinaitic Covenant tells the Jew what to do and how to act as a member of the covenantal community, the Patriarchic Covenant addresses the "I" awareness of the Jew, teaching him how to experience his Jewishness. It sensitizes him in specifically Jewish ways; it expresses attitudes, ideals, and sentiments which still speak to us. It guides our feelings and consciousness rather than our physical acts, for we are duty-bound not only to act as Jews, but to feel as Jews. In a word, it is the backdrop of the Sinaitic Covenant; the latter is the behavioral fulfillment of the truths, values, and Jewish self-awareness established by the former.

Abraham, the idol-wrecker, pleads peace with Lot (13:8) but goes to war to rescue him (14:14). To strangers, his hand is open (18:1) and, in the name of Divine justice, he intercedes for Sodom and Gomorrah (18:23). Sarah's perceptive wisdom regarding Ishmael draws Divine approval (21:12). Our sages teach: "Our father Abraham was tested with ten trials (of faith and character) and he withstood them all, demonstrating the extent of Abraham's love of God" (Av. 5:4).[8] These ten trials, with the climactic *Akedah* as the supreme expression of martyrdom, are the source of many Jewish traits which are still prevalent amongst our people. In studying their life experiences with Aggadic elaboration during our impressionable childhood and throughout our adult years, we absorb their values and nuances of feeling into our Jewish consciousness. "Every Jew should ask himself, 'when shall my deeds be like those of Abraham, Isaac, and Jacob?' " (*Tanna d'bei Eliyahu Rabbah* 25).[9]

Our Sages suggest that the lives of the patriarchs portray the total historical experience of our people. "God gave Abraham a sign that whatever happened to him would occur to his descendants" (*Tanḥuma, Lekh Lekha* 9).[10] Naḥmanides adds: "It is for this reason that the verses narrate at great length the account of the journeys, the digging of the wells, and the other events. . . . in truth, they serve as a lesson of the future."[11] Thus, all of Jewish history and the basic character of the Jew was shaped by the covenantal period of the patriarchs. Their life-experiences still nourish our self-consciousness as Jews even as the Sinaitic Covenant guides the format of our lives.

[The next three chapters provide insights derived from the Patriarchic Covenantal period.]

הערות לפרק 6

1 **דברים כט, יג**: ולא אתכם לבדכם אנכי כרת את הברית הזאת — פ' רש"י — ואף עם דורות העתידים להיות (יד).

2 **סוף הקדמת הרמב"ם למשנה תורה**: ומנין מצות התורה הנוהגות לדורות, שש מאות ושלש עשרה מצות (תרי"ג) מהם מצות "עשה" מאתים וארבעים ושמונה (רמ"ח), סימן להן — מנין אבריו של אדם. ומהן מצות "לא תעשה" שלש מאות וששים וחמש (שס"ה), סימן להן מנין ימי שנת החמה (ראה רמב"ם, ס' המצות, מצוה א).

3 **רש"י שמות כה, טז**: שהיא לעדות ביני וביניכם שצויתי אתכם מצות הכתובות בה.

4 **בראשית יז, יא**: ונמלתם את בשר ערלתכם והיה לאות ברית ביני וביניכם. ראה ס' החנוך (ב) — אות קבוע בגופם להבדילם משאר העמים.

5 **ויקרא כו, מב**: וזכרתי את בריתי יעקוב ואף את בריתי יצחק ואף את בריתי אברהם אזכור והארץ אזכור.

6 **שם מה**: וזכרתי להם ברית ראשונים אשר הוצאתי אותם מארץ מצרים. רש"י — של שבטים; אבן עזרא — זאת הברית הכרותה בסיני; ספרא — ברית סיני.

7 **שבת ל ע"א**: כשחטאו ישראל במדבר, עמד משה לפני הקב"ה ואמר כמה תפלות ותחנונים לפניו ולא נענה. וכשאמר, זכור לאברהם ליצחק ולישראל עבדיך, מיד נענה.

8 **אבות ה, ד**: עשרה נסיונות נתנסה אברהם אבינו ועמד בכולם, להודיע כמה חבתו של אברהם אבינו.

9 **תנא דבי אליהו רבה פכ"ה**: מתי יגיעו מעשי למעשי אברהם יצחק ויעקב.

10 **תנחומא לך לך, ט**: סימן נתן לו הקב"ה לאברהם שכל מה שאירע בו, אירע לבניו.

11 **רמב"ן בראשית יב, ו**: אומר לך כלל, תבין אותו בכל הפרשיות הבאות בענין אברהם, יצחק ויעקב. והוא ענין גדול הזכירוהו רבותינו בדרך קצרה ואמרו כל מה שאירע לאבות סימן לבנים, ולכך יאריכו הכתובים בספור המסעות וחפירת הבארות ושאר המקרים, ויחשוב החושב בהם כאלו הם דברים מיותרים, אין בהם תועלת, וכולם באים ללמד על העתיד (ראה רמב"ן סוף ספר בראשית).

CHAPTER VII

DESTINY, NOT CAUSALITY, GOVERNS JEWISH HISTORY

The Patriarchic Covenant introduced a new concept into history. While universal (non-Jewish) history is governed by *causality,* by what preceded, covenantal (Jewish) history is shaped by *destiny,* by a goal set in the future.

Universal history is of an etiological nature; every event is brought about by a preceding cause. Event A occurs and B follows, or, colloquially speaking, A begets B. Such history develops almost mechanically, origins determine events; the present is precipitated by the past. Most historians are guided by this principle, namely, that causality (or high probability) dictates unfolding events. When secular scholars try to interpret Jewish history in this manner, they inevitably arrive at bizarre conclusions and distortions.

Covenantal Jewish history, by contrast, is teleological, not etiological. This means that it is propelled by a purpose. What happens to Jews emanates from a Divine promise foretold about the future, rather than by events impelling from the past. Jewish history is pulled, as by a magnet, towards a glorious destiny; it is not pushed by antecedent causes. This is the meaning of the Patriarchic Covenant; it is a goal projected, a purpose pursued, a destination to be reached.

For example, the modern worldwide efforts of the Jewish people to sustain and secure the State of Israel despite almost total world opposition is a purely covenantal experience. The passionate, almost irrational determination to establish a Jewish state cannot be explained, as some scholars have attempted to do, as a variation of the nationalistic ferment which gripped many Western European peoples in the nineteenth century or even as a reaction to the horrors of the Holocaust, which destroyed one-third of our people. Such explanations cannot account for the intensity and solidarity of the American Jew, who is ready to jeopardize his political and economic status in American society, if need be, for the sake of Israel's survival and well-being. Other nations have suffered lesser catastrophes and have succumbed to the imperatives of historical decline. Not so with the Jew, who emerged out of the Holocaust, not depressed and distraught from the blows of the past, but energized with superhuman zealousness by a dream about the future which the flames of the crematoria could not extinguish.

In the hearts of most Jews, there is an awareness that Israel is a promised land. The promise, a destiny to be fulfilled, is the cause of present exertions; it is not the result of a conglomeration of past events. The drive for Israel is fueled by anticipation, by something beautiful and miraculous which defies precise formulation, which hovers and beckons on the distant horizon. Even secular Zionists, who formally decry all religious terminology and motivations, often speak with Messianic overtones. Destiny, not causality, constitutes the dynamics of covenantal history. The future is responsible for the past.

Destiny and Destination

The word "destiny" is etymologically related to the word "destination." What determines Jewish historical experience is not one's point of departure, but one's destination. There are two types of travelers. Some merely wander about restlessly, unable to stay put in any one place and going nowhere in particular. Circumstances dictate their movement. An experienced traveler, however, has a destination to which he is rushing, and he wants to get there as soon as possible. And that is precisely the factor that shapes Jewish history, which is unlike the histories of other nations. The Jew is rushing somewhere, and, however, often he is sidetracked, he returns to resume the journey.

What is the destination of the Jew? Where is it on the map? It is the eschatological redemption, *ketz ha-yamim,* not only of the Jew and mankind, but of the entire universe, as the prophet foretold: "The Lord shall be king over all the earth (*malkhut shamayim*—universal religion); in that day shall the Lord be One and His Name One" (Zech. 14:9).[1] This is the Messianic dream of Judaism and the spiritual goal of Jewish history.

The Patriarchic Covenant created this new concept of historical destiny. It promised Israel a faith, a land, and a future redemption. It pledged, "And I shall make of thee a great nation, and I will bless thee and make thy name great, and thou shalt be a blessing . . . and all the families of the earth shall bless themselves through you" (Gen. 12:2–3).[2] It forged a people with a great destination.

הערות לפרק 7

1 **זכריה יד, ט**: והיה ה' למלך על כל הארץ, ביום ההוא יהיה ה' אחד ושמו אחד.

2 **בראשית יב, ב-ג**: ואעשך לגוי גדול, ואברכך ואגדלה שמך, והיה ברכה... ונברכו בך כל משפחות האדמה.

Chapter VIII

THE UNIVERSAL AND THE COVENANTAL

There are religiously committed Jews who are indifferent to the concerns of the larger non-Jewish society. They are content to reside in isolated communities with unconcern, if not actual disdain, for the Gentile world and for the problems which afflict humanity. This introversion can be explained as a reaction to the centuries-old derision and persecution which have been the Jewish historical experience and to which they were subjected with particular ferocity in modern times. Nowadays, there are particular aspects of moral perversion afflicting the general society which are repellant to Jewish sensibilities. Nevertheless, this insularity cannot be vindicated as authentic Judaism even if it can be understood and justified in particular historical periods and situations.

The Messianic Fulfillment

The fullest realization of Jewish history will be achieved in Messianic days. The Jewish vision of the Messianic era includes tranquility and fulfillment for all mankind, not only for the Jewish people. The Yalkut writes: "Every people or nation which did not oppress Israel will partake of the Messianic era" (*Bo*, 212).[1] A universal brotherhood will accompany a restored and vindicated Israel, and a worldwide regeneration was foretold by the prophet Zechariah: "And the Lord shall be king over all the earth; in that day shall the Lord be one and His Name one" (14:9).[2] Isaiah elaborated on this universal theme: "And many peoples shall go and say: Come, let us go up the

Mount of the Lord, to the House of the God of Jacob, and He will teach us His ways and we will walk in his paths" (2:3).³

King Solomon was solicitous of the welfare of Gentiles who would come to pray at the Temple: "If a foreigner who is not of Your people Israel comes from a distant land for the sake of Your Name, for they shall hear about Your great Name and Your mighty hand and Your outstretched arm—when he comes to pray toward this House, Oh, hear in Your heavenly abode and grant all that the foreigner asks of You. Thus, all peoples of the earth will know Your Name and revere You as does Your people, Israel. And they will acknowledge that Your Name is attached to this house that I have built" (I Kings 8:41–43).⁴

Sacrificial offerings on behalf of the nations of the world predominated during the Sukkot festival (Num. R. 21:22),⁵ and our liturgy, particularly during the High Holy Days, abounds with universal themes. Even as the Jew is moved by his private Sinaitic Covenant with God to embody and preserve the teachings of the Torah, he is committed to the belief that all mankind, of whatever color or creed, is "in His image" and is possessed of an inherent human dignity and worthiness. Man's singularity is derived from the breath "He [God] breathed into his nostrils" at the moment of creation (Gen. 2:7). Thus, we do share in the universal historical experience, and God's providential concern does embrace all of humanity.

Abraham's Experience

We study the narratives of the patriarchal period as though these early Jews were lifted out of the ordinary concerns which affected their non-Jewish neighbors. In fact, there is no purely covenantal historical experience. The reason is obvious. Abraham lived among various people of divergent faiths. When he negotiated with the sons of Heth (of the Hittites) for a burial plot for his wife, Sarah, he defined his status: "I am a stranger [immigrant] and a resident among you" (Gen. 23:4).⁶ He was basically declaring that the sectarian faith he was propounding did not preclude his commitment to further the welfare of the general society. Indeed, the Midrash teaches: "Great are the righteous for occupying themselves with the habitation of the world."[7]

When the wayward cities of Sodom and Gomorrah were threatened with Divine retribution, Abraham perseveringly intervened in their behalf, lest the righteous few be undeservingly punished (Gen. 18:23). He had Amorite friends—Aner, Eshcol, and Mamre—who were his allies in the war to rescue Lot (14:13)[8] and with whom he consulted on important matters (Rashi 18:1).[9]

The modern Jew is entangled in the activities of the Gentile society in numerous ways—economically, politically, culturally, and, on some levels, socially. We share in the universal experience. The problems of humanity, war and peace, political stability or anarchy, morality or permissiveness, famine, epidemics, and pollution transcend the boundaries of ethnic groups. A stricken environment, both physical and ideological, can wreak havoc upon all groups.

The responsibility of subduing the forces of nature and converting them into life-supportive energies was directed to Adam, the progenitor of all mankind. On the verse "rule over the fish of the sea . . . and subdue it" (Gen. 1:26–28), Naḥmanides adds: "He gave them [mankind] the power and the dominion over the earth to do as they wish with the cattle, the reptiles, and all that crawl in the dust, and to build and to pluck up that which was planted, and from the hills, to dig copper and other similar things."[10] This commandment was addressed to all the descendants of Adam, Jew and non-Jew alike. All are mandated to harness the forces of nature for the betterment of mankind. Jewish concerns are not exclusively parochial. It is our duty as human beings to contribute our energies and creativity to alleviate the pressing needs and anguish of mankind and to contribute to its welfare.

The Burial Cave of Kiryat Arba

The Torah tells us that the city of Hebron was also called Kiryat Arba (lit., City of the Four) (Gen. 23:2). Rashi explains: "It was so called because of the four couples who were buried there, man and wife: Adam and Eve, Abraham and Sarah, Isaac and Rebecca, Jacob and Leah."[11] Why, we ask, were our great patriarchs and matriarchs, founders of our people, buried in the same cave with Adam and Eve, who were the progenitors of all mankind? Apparently, there is no gap between Adam and Even and the patriarchs. Human dignity, exemplified by Adam and Eve, who were created in God's image (1:27), and covenantal sanctity, which was introduced by the patriarchs, are not mutually exclusive. Man—all humankind—possesses worthiness because he reflects in human measure such divine attributes as intellect, free will, and a moral sense.

The psalmist extols man's uniqueness: "Thou hast made him but a little lower than the angels and hast crowned him with glory and honor. Thou hast made him to have dominion over the works of Thy hands" (8:6–7).[12] Rabbinic interpretation of the covenant God made with Noah (Gen. 9) deduced the Seven Noahide Laws whose observance is obligatory for all Gentiles, while the Jew is enjoined to fulfill a more stringent and demanding discipline. Gentiles governed by those seven laws are judged worthy of eternal life. These are: establishment of courts of justice (precluding anarchy), prohibition of blasphemy, of idolatry, of incest, of bloodshed, robbery, and eating flesh cut from a living animal (Sanh. 56a).[13] These fundamental precepts require proper actions rather than beliefs and are vital to the existence of a moral society.

Abraham did not appear in the historical arena in order to free the Jew from universal obligations. On the contrary, the covenant enhances the universal norm and elevates it to greater heights. It adds many more norms to those obligatory upon all members of mankind. The Talmud teaches: "There is nothing that is permitted to the Jew that is forbidden to the sons of Noah" (Sanh. 59).[14] Rashi adds: "When Jews became differentiated from the sons of Noah, it was to sanctify themselves [with additional duties] and not to lighten their responsibilities."

Sanctity, the goal of the Torah discipline, involves an additional dimension. It bids the Jew to imitate God, *imitatio dei,* "Be you holy because I, the Lord your God, am holy" (Lev. 19:2).[15] Our Sages frequently refer to God as "the Holy One, blessed is He," *Hakadosh barukh hu.* The root word *k-d-sh* means to set apart, to separate and thereby to hallow, to consecrate, to sanctify. It bids one to be aloof from the banal, the impure, the profane, and the sensual. Isaiah's vision heard the angels singing to God: "Holy, Holy, Holy is the Lord of Hosts! His presence fills the earth" (6:3),[16] signifying that holiness is His essence. The Jewish people is mandated through the Commandments of the Torah to reach for the ideal of being "a kingdom of priests and a *holy* nation" (Ex. 19:6),[17] to imitate God here on earth by elevating the earthly to a higher spiritual purpose.

There is no contradiction between laws rooted in the universal *imageo dei* (God's image), the source of man's dignity which mandates the Seven Noahide Laws, and those rooted in sanctity, *kedushah,* which was introduced through the covenant. Non-Jews, however, even those well-intentioned, are frequently unable to appreciate that the covenant is not neglectful of universal concerns. They would feel more comfortable, they intimate, if the Jew would limit himself only to the concerns of the general community. This misunderstanding results in inevitable tensions.

Abraham's Contribution

What precisely did Abraham introduce that was strange to his contemporaries? What does holiness mean?

The first ten generations of mankind, which culminated with the flood, *dor hamabul,* emphasized the pleasure principle, the exhilaration of the senses, as the primary goal of life. This, according to Maimonides, constituted the sin of the first couple in partaking of "the tree which was good [pleasing] for food and a delight to the eyes" (Gen. 3:6; Guide 1:2).[18] The aesthetic-pleasure experience is a boundless experience, reaching out without restraint or discipline. It regards ethics as irrelevant and all barriers or authority as repressive. "I do what I like, whatever is pleasant." The fleeting sensation of the moment is primary; future consequences are dismissed. The Western world partakes considerably of the philosophy of the *dor hamabul*.

Such a value system invites moral decay. Cain killed Abel, Lamech boasted of his crimes (Gen. 4:23), and "the aristocratic sons" *b'nai he-elohim* (Targum, Rashi), flouted all morality by expropriating for sensual pleasure the wives of the common folk and indulged in pederasty and bestiality (Rashi, Gen. 6:2).[19] Rampant predators and moral anarchy ensued as society "became corrupt and the land was filled with violence [*ḥamas*] . . . all flesh perverted its way on the earth" (ibid. 6:11–12).[20] The flood was inevitable.

The next ten generations, *dor haflagah* (the generation of dispersion), were symbolized by the abortive attempt to build the Tower of Babel (chap. 11). Not pleasure but power, to control nature through technology, to enthrone man as the master of the universe and to dispose of God's sovereignty and His worship—these defined their primary motivations.

Theirs was an organized society with professed "love and friendship for each other" (Rashi 11:9), yet repressively conformative, all of "one language and of few words" (11:1). Nimrod, their leader, was a formidable trapper who ensnared the minds of his generation through propaganda (Rashi 10:9), to fight religion and to further his imperialistic ambition (10:10). The tower symbolizes their ambition "to ascend to the skies and to do battle with Him." (Rashi 11:1) Technology was prized over human life, as portrayed by the Midrash. In building the tower, they bemoaned the loss of a falling brick, but if a worker fell to his death, they were unperturbed because he was easily replaced.[21] Society and ideology were primary; individuals were expendable.

While the *dor hamabul* was filled with brigands, the *dor hafplagah* conducted a tightly controlled society with religion suppressed and human life devalued. Communist society is the *dor haflagah;* the dissolution of its hegemony is inevitable.

Abraham offered a new vision of man's purpose and destiny. Not wallowing in pleasure or the arrogance of power, but clinging to God, to find Him and to please Him—these were man's primary purpose. As He is holy, so should we be, even if it involves discipline, withdrawal, and sacrifice, even if it circumscribes one's range of permissible behavior. Pleasure and power are man-centered and do not respond to a higher authority; *kedushah* is God-centered and it acknowledges Divine rulership.

Kedushah has an antithetical quality. It frightens many whose ego and ambition are at the center of their universe. They resist the stirrings of their soul as they deny the mystery of man's uniqueness on earth. Such desensitized people are daunted and repelled by *kedushah* and by the self-discipline it demands.

However, for people with imaginative perception and intellectual honesty, *kedushah* is fascinating. One feels pulled, as by a magnet, to the Creator, the *Boré Olam,* unconsciously, almost instinctively; "as the gazelle which panteth after brooks of water, so panteth my soul after thee, O God" (Ps. 42:2).[22] Why the comparison with a gazelle? In the jungle, late in the afternoon, animals begin their march towards streams and brooks. They have no memories of accumulated experience. How do they know their way? Or, birds flying southward, guided and driven by an inner propulsion until they reach their destination.

So is man drawn to the Divine Creator, unconsciously, not necessarily the result of any philosophy. This was the religious quest of Abraham from which he derived *kedushah* as the primary purpose of life. The resurgence and persistence of religious yearning in modern times, despite years of scientific secularism, reflects the irrepressible search of the gazelle for brooks of refreshing water.

Abraham and Ishmael

Abraham walked with Ishmael and Isaac towards Mount Moriah, the site of Isaac's intended sacrifice and the locale of the future Temple. "On the third day, Abraham looked up and saw the place from afar. Abraham said to the young men [Ishmael and others]: 'Stay here, *poh,* with the donkey. The boy [Isaac] and I will go up there, *koh.* We will worship and then return to you' " (22:4–5).[23]

Abraham, in a precise and prophetic manner, suggested the tension and fundamental difference in the destination of the non-Jew and the Jew, between Ishmael and Isaac. The word *poh* ("here") reflects the universal commitment, which was as far as Ishmael was to go. Seven commandments were given to the descendants of Noah which are incumbent on all mankind. The word *koh,* in our context, can only mean "there" (*sham*), namely, the seat of holiness, the Temple site. The Jew must go beyond *poh* and endeavor to arrive at *koh.*

The non-Jew does not comprehend the difference between *poh* and *koh.* "Why is the Jew so restless," they ask, "always pursuing goals beyond those which concern us?" They don't appreciate that it is the sanctity of Mount Moriah, the higher ideals of spiritual attainment, which beckons the Jew to go beyond the *poh.* The fact, however, that so many non-Jews fail to comprehend the extended destination mandated by the covenant, a chosenness which is not rejectionist, will not deflect us from our journey to *koh.* We will continue to affirm the worthiness of traveling with the patriarchs, despite the additional burdens the journey entails.

הערות לפרק 8

1. **ילקוט שמעוני פ׳ בא, ריב**: כל גוי וכל ממלכה שלא ענו את ישראל ולא לחצו אותם באין לימות המשיח.

2. **זכריה יד, ט**: והיה ה׳ למלך על כל הארץ, ביום ההוא יהיה ה׳ אחד ושמו אחד. פי׳ רש״י, שיהא שמו נזכר בפי כולם; פי׳ מצודת דוד, אז כל העכו״ם יקבלוהו לאלוה ויאמינו בו.

3 **ישעיה ב, ג:** והלכו עמים רבים ואמרו לכו ונעלה אל הר ה', אל בית אלקי יעקב ויורנו מדרכיו ונלכה בארוחותיו. כי מציון תצא תורה ודבר ה' מירושלים.

4 **מלכים א' ח, מא-מג:** וגם אל הנכרי אשר לא מעמך ישראל הוא, ובא מארץ רחוקה למען שמך. כי ישמעון את שמך הגדול ואת ידך החזקה וזרועיך הנטויה, ובא והתפלל אל הבית הזה, אתה תשמע השמים מכון שבתך ועשית ככל אשר יקרא אליך הנכרי, למען ידעון כל עמי הארץ את שמך ליראה אותך כעמך ישראל ולדעת כי שמך נקרא על הבית הזה אשר בניתי.

5 **במד"ר כא, כב:** ביום השמיני עצרת (במדבר כט, לה), זש"ה תחת אהבתי ישטנוני ואני תפלה (תהלים קט, ד); את מוצא בחג, ישראל מקריבין לפניך ע' פרים על ע' אומות. אמרו ישראל, רבון העולמים, הרי אנו מקריבים עליהם ע' פרים והיו צריכין לאהוב אותנו, והם תחת אהבתי ישטנוני, לפיכך א"ל הקב"ה, עכשיו הקריבו על עצמכם, ביום השמיני עצרת תהיה לכם.

6 **בראשית כג, ג-ד:** וידבר אל בני חת לאמר, גר ותושב אנכי עמכם.

7 **מדרש חפץ:** וישב יצחק ויחפור את בארות המים (בראשית כו, יח), גדולין הצדיקים שהם עוסקים בישוב העולם (מלאכת מחשבת).

8 **בראשית יד, יג:** והוא שוכן באלוני ממרא האמורי, אחי אשכול ואחי ענר והם בעלי ברית אברם. פי' רש"י, שכרתו עמו ברית; בלעדי רק אשר אכלו הנערים, וחלק האנשים אשר הלכו אתי, ענר אשכול וממרא, הם יקחו חלקם (בראשית יד, כד).

9 **שם יח, א:** וירא אליו ה' באלוני ממרא. פי' רש"י, הוא שנתן לו עצה על המילה, לפיכך נגלה עליו בחלקו.

10 **שם א, כו:** וירדו בדגת הים ובעוף השמים ובבהמה ובכל הארץ . . . וכבשוה. פי' רמב"ן, נתן להם כח וממשלה בארץ לעשות כרצונם בבהמות ובשרצים ובכל זוחלי עפר ולבנות ולעקור נטוע ומהרריה לחצוב נחשת וכיוצא בזה.

11 **שם כג, ב:** ותמת שרה בקרית ארבע היא חברון. פי' רש"י, על שם ארבע זוגות שנקברו שם, איש ואשתו, אדם וחוה, אברהם ושרה, יצחק ורבקה, יעקב ולאה.

12 **תהלים ח, ו-ז:** ותחסרהו מעט מאלקים וכבוד והדר תעטרהו. תמשילהו במעשי ידיך כל שתה תחת רגליו.

13 **סנהדרין נו ע"א:** שבע מצוות נצטוו בני נח: דינים, וברכת השם, עבודה זרה, גלוי עריות ושפיכות דמים וגזל ואבר מן החי.

14 **סנהדרין נט ע"א:** ליכא מידעם דלישראל שרי ולבני נח אסור. פי' רש"י, שכשיצאו מכלל בני נח להתקדש יצאו ולא להקל עליהם.

15 **ויקרא יט, ב:** קדושים תהיו כי קדוש אני ה' אלקיכם. פי' רש"י, הוי פרושים מן העריות ומן העבירה.

16 **ישעיה ו, ג**: וקרא זה אל זה ואמר: קדוש, קדוש, קדוש ה׳ צבאות, מלא כל הארץ כבודו.

17 **שמות יט, ו**: ואתם תהיו לי ממלכת כהנים וגוי קדוש.

18 **רמב״ם. מורה א, ב**: וכאשר חטא ונטה אחרי תאוותיו הדמיוניות ותענוגות חושיו הגופניים כמו שנאמר כי טוב העץ למאכל וכי תאוה הוא לעינים, נענש שנשללה ממנו אותה ההשגה השכלית, ולפיכך המרה את הצווי אשר מחמת שכלו נצטווה בו (תרגום יוסף קאפח).

19 **בראשית ו, ב**: מכל אשר בחרו. פי׳ רש״י: אף בעולת בעל, אף הזכר והבהמה.

20 **שם ו, יא-יב**: ותשחת הארץ לפני האלקים ותמלא הארץ חמס . . . כי השחית כל בשר את דרכו על הארץ.

21 אם נפל אדם ומת לא היו שמים את לבם אליו, ואם נפלה לבנה אחת היו יושבים ובוכים (פדר״א, כד).

22 **תהלים מב, ב**: כאיל תערוג על אפיקי מים, נפשי תערוג אליך אלקים.

23 **בראשית כב, ד-ה**: ביום השלישי וישא אברהם את עיניו וירא את המקום מרחוק. ויאמר אברהם אל נעריו, שבו לכם פה עם החמור ואני והנער נלכה עד כה ונשתחוה ונשובה אליכם.

CHAPTER IX

THE COVENANTAL ROLE OF SARAH

The Torah and its Midrashic elaboration provide us with extensive information about the patriarchs. The matriarchic role, however, is relatively obscure. In fact, Sarah was an equal and indispensable partner of Abraham in the covenant and in the propagation of the faith. When they started their travels, the Torah relates that Abraham took "the souls they had made in Haran" (Gen. 12:5). How does one make souls? Rashi explains: "This refers to the souls they had brought into the faith. Abraham converted the men, and Sarah converted the women, and the Torah accounts it as if they had made them."[1] So successful were their missionary efforts that "they gathered unto their fold thousands and tens of thousands who became part of the household of Abraham" (Maimonides, Hil. Avodah Zarah 1:3).[2]

Commenting on the verse "I will remember My covenant with Jacob as well as My covenant with Isaac, and also My covenant with Abraham I will remember" (Lev. 26:42), our Sages ask: "We note here a covenant with the patriarchs. How do we know that the matriarchs were also part of the covenant? This is derived from the redundant word *et* [which in the verse precedes the name of each of the patriarchs and is not needed grammatically; the preposition *et* is usually interpreted by our Sages as intending an extended meaning and application]." The word *et* in our verse suggests the inclusion of the matriarchs, as in the verse: "This is where Abraham was buried and [*v'et*] Sarah his wife" (Gen. 49:31; Lev. R. 36:4).[3]

Abraham's role is more explicitly indicated because it was he who was active in public life. When the angels asked Abraham, "Where is your wife, Sarah?" he replied, "Here in the tent" (Gen. 18:9), to which Rashi appends, "The ministering angels knew, indeed, where our mother Sarah was, but they asked this question in order to call attention to her modesty [retiring disposition] and so to endear her all the more to her husband . . . she was a private person."[4] The Talmud adds further: "From here we learn that the private role is honorable for a woman" (Yev. 77).[5] Sarah's manner was regarded as praiseworthy.

In Proverbs (31), Solomon extolled the exemplary woman who "looks well after her household" and "whose husband is known in the gates, when he sits among the elders of the land." In some matters of a personal and family nature, Sarah's spiritual discernment is praised as being superior to Abraham's. When her husband hesitated about sending away Hagar and Ishmael because of Ishmael's baneful influence upon her son Isaac, God said to Abraham, "All that Sarah says to you, listen to her voice" (Gen. 21:12).[6] Rashi adds, "We may infer that Abraham was inferior to Sarah in respect of prophecy."

The Existential Equality of Man and Woman

The foremost distinguishing characteristic bestowed upon man is his Divine image, his *tzelem Elohim,* which denotes particular qualitative endowments, such as a moral sense, free will, and intellect. Man partakes of these attributes within human limitations, while God's representation of these qualities is absolute. Maimonides embodied man's likeness to God primarily in terms of his intellect (Guide 1:1). This Divine gift was given to both men and women. "And God created man with His image. In the image of God, He created him; male and female He created them" (Gen. 1:27).[7] In their spiritual natures, they were equally worthy.

Two humans were created who differ from each other metaphysically, not only physiologically, even as they both partake of Divine qualities. This contradicts the perverse notion that Judaism regards woman as being inferior to man. It also cuts away another false notion that there is no distinction between them in terms of their spiritual personalities. Two sexes were formed not only for propagative purposes, but they constitute existential originals. They differ in their psychical natures.

Yet, even as we recognize metaphysical differences, we insist that they do not differ axiologically, as regards their worthiness before God. Both bear His image, which is the ultimate criterion of value; both may be "called to the colors" to assume leadership roles, as history-makers, as God's messengers. Sarah, Miriam, Deborah, Esther, and many others whom Scripture has relegated to anonymity, were elected by Providence as *shelihay hakel,* His emissaries when great problems were to be overcome. God created a dual human existence, man and woman, because they complement one another. They represent two existential destinies; together, they form one destiny, a more perfect one.

No Covenant Without Sarah

The significant role of Sarah is indicated when Abraham, despairing of having a child with Sarah, wondered whether God intended that the heritage be transmitted through Ishmael. "And Abraham said to God: 'May it be granted that Ishmael live before You.' " God replied: "But [*aval*] your wife Sarah will bear you a son, and you shall call him Isaac, and I will keep My covenant with him as an everlasting treaty, for his descendants after him" (Gen. 17:18).[8] The key emphasis is in the word *aval.* God is explaining that His covenant cannot be realized without Isaac. Why? Because Isaac is the son of Sarah, *aval Sarah ishtekha yoledet.* Isaac will emerge out of both of you, but Ishmael is only derived from you. And there can be no covenant without Sarah.

Further indication of Sarah's equal participation in the covenant is suggested in the verses informing Abraham that his wife's name was changed from Sarai to Sarah. "God said to Abraham: "Sarai your wife—do not call her by the name Sarai, for Sarah is her name" (ibid. 17:15).[9] He is *not* informed that henceforth her name will be Sarah but that it *is* Sarah, suggesting that she had acquired this name previously, *ki Sarah shemah*. This subtlety in language is apparent when we compare it to God's command to Abraham about his own name change: "No longer shall you be called Abram. Your name shall become [henceforth] Abraham" (v. 5).[10] In Sarah's case, the word "is" refers to an earlier change, but in Abraham's name-change, the words "shall become" suggest that an order is now going into effect.

But when was her name changed? The answer is, at the very moment when Abraham's name was changed. There was an existential interdependence between both. The name change of both involved the addition of a letter from God's name, the Tetragrammaton, signifying that they will share a spiritual role which will reach out unto the nations of the world. He was to become an *av hamon goyim,* "the father of a multitude of nations" (Gen. 17:4) and she "a princess to the entire world" (Rashi, ibid., 17:15; Ber. 13a). Abraham could not be "a father of multitudes" if Sarah were not crowned as a "mother" of this multitude.[11]

In a word, not only did man and woman achieve human dignity together at creation, both in God's image, but they also attained together, and only together, covenantal sanctity, being elected by God to be the founders of a new faith.

Their covenantal interdependence is further indicated by the fact that the Torah does not dwell on Abraham's life after Sarah's death. Though he survived her by many years, he knew that his mission as the father of the covenantal community was concluded, and that from that point, all he had to do was to act out the last part of the drama and walk off the covenantal stage and make room for someone else to succeed him. Only two items remained for him to complete: to purchase the Cave of

Machpelah as a burial place for Sarah (Gen. 23:3) and to arrange for the marriage of his son Isaac.

The latter story is told not to portray the story of Abraham, but to acquaint us with the second mother of the covenantal community, Rebecca, who succeeded Sarah. The concluding verse of this episode clearly informs us that the vacancy was filled. "And Isaac brought [Rebecca] into his mother Sarah's tent and he married her. She became his wife and he loved her. Isaac was then consoled for the loss of his mother" (24:67).[12] Now the covenant could be resumed, because there was a mother, not only a father, in the covenantal leadership. Nothing more is told to us about Abraham's life after Sarah's death because with Sarah's death, the covenant came to a temporary halt.

Mourning and Weeping for Sarah

The above may explain the manner of Abraham's mourning at Sarah's death. "And Abraham came to mourn for Sarah [*lispod*, eulogize] and to weep for her [*livkotah*]" (23:2).[13] Weeping and mourning are two different stages in bereavement. Weeping is a primeval, instinctive reaction to a tragedy, especially one that strikes without warning. It is not a deliberate performance; it bursts forth spontaneously. Weeping is a release of unbearable tension when the whole world seems to be crumbling.

Mourning, *hesped,* in contrast, is a rational and planned performance. It is an act of appraisal, an attempt to evaluate the repercussions of what has transpired. A *hesped* is formulated not in emotional terms, but in logical analysis.

With the death of Sarah, Abraham had suffered a double loss. First was his personal sorrow, the death of his wife, his partner and comrade. No one can understand the bleak loneliness and painful nostalgia of a surviving mate. One's whole world seems dislocated. Abraham was a great human being, and he felt profoundly disoriented; his beloved Sarah was gone.

Another tragic and distressful experience was his dilemma as to what would now become of the covenant which was the *raison d'être* of all his strivings. He knew the secret that it was not entrusted to him alone. What would happen now? The mother of the covenant was missing. Would God have confidence in him alone, or was his life's work now coming to an end?

The first thing he did was to appraise Sarah's contribution, *lispod et Sarah,* to review the formation and successful growth of the covenantal community, the role she had played and what she had accomplished. He mourned her departure together with many thousands of other adherents of the covenant who had adopted the faith. He mourned the passing of a great woman in objective categories. Only after the evaluative presentation did Abraham break down in tears and cry. Others could identify with his *hesped,* but no one could share his personal pain.

What Was Sarah Like?

A characterization of Sarah is implicit in the verse which records her passing. "The life of Sarah was a hundred years and twenty years and seven years; these were the years of Sarah's life" (Gen. 23:1).[14] Rashi takes note of the redundant word "years" after each number and explains that at a hundred, Sarah was as sinless as she was at twenty, and she was as robustly beautiful at twenty as she was at seven.

Rashi also notes the seemingly superfluous words: "These were the years of Sarah's life," *shnei ḥayyei Sarah.* What do these words mean? The word "years" would not refer to the numerical span of Sarah's life, for the verse has already indicated that she lived 127 years. Rather, Rashi says, it is to be understood in a qualitative sense. "They [all her years, at seven, at twenty, at a hundred] were equally good," *kulan shavin l'tovah.* What kind of person was this regal woman, and what constituted the uniqueness of her personality?

Rashi is suggesting that the three divisions of life—childhood, youth, and adulthood—need not be mutually exclusive. One can retain the positive strengths of past stages even as we progress in life. The charismatic covenantal personality—indeed, this is the mark of true greatness—is able to absorb and to experience the qualities of three periods simultaneously.

The child is endowed with a capacity of an all-absorbing faith and trustfulness; youth bursts with zealousness, idealism, and optimism; the adult, mellowed with years, has the benefit of accumulated knowledge and dispassionate judgment. Each age is physically and psychologically attuned to particular emphases, but the superior individual can retain and harmonize the positive strengths of all three periods during his entire lifetime.

Sarah was such a person, "the goodness of her life was equally distributed," *kulan shavim l'tovah*. She was at the same time a child in her total faith, youthful in her exuberant idealism and an adult in the maturity of her judgment. This was the tribute Abraham bestowed on Sarah.

הערות לפרק 9

1 **בראשית יב, ה**: ואת הנפש אשר עשו בחרן — פי' רש"י, שהכניסן תחת כנפי השכינה, אברהם מגיר את האנשים ושרה מגירת הנשים ומעלה עליהם הכתוב כאלו עשאום (לכך כתיב אשר עשו).

2 **רמב"ם הל' ע"ז פ"א ה"ג**: וכיון שהיו העם מתקבצים אליו ושואלים לו על דבריו, היה מודיע לכל אחד ואחד כפי דעתו עד שיחזירהו לדרך האמת, עד שנתקבצו אליו אלפים ורבבות והם אנשי בית אברהם. ושתל בלבם העיקר הגדול הזה (שורש האמונה באל עולם אחד ואפסות האלילים).

3 **ויקרא כו, מב**: וזכרתי את בריתי יעקב ואף את בריתי יצחק ואף את בריתי אברהם והארץ אזכור — ויק"ר לו, ד — אין לי אלא אבות, אמהות מנין? ת"ל, את, את, את. אין אתים אלא אמהות דכתי', "שמה קברו את אברהם ואת שרה אשתו" (בראשית מט, לא).

4 **בראשית יח, ט**: ויאמרו אליו, איה שרה אשתך? ויאמר הנה באהל — פי' רש"י, יודעים היו מלאכי השרת שרה אמנו היכן היתה אלא להודיע שצנועה היתה, כדי לחבבה על בעלה (ב"מ פ"ז).

5 **יבמות עז**: מכאן כל כבודה בת מלך פנימה (דכבודה של אשה לשבת בבית).

6 **בראשית כא, יב**: כל אשר תאמר אליך שרה, שמע בקולה — פי׳ רש״י — למדנו שהיה אברהם טפל לשרה בנביאות (דאל״כ, לא היה הקב״ה מרשה לאברהם לשמוע בקולה בלא גבול וקצבה, פי׳ ת״ת).

7 **בראשית א, כז**: ויברא אלקים את האדם בצלמו, בצלם אלקים ברא אותו, זכר ונקבה ברא אותם.

8 **שם יז, יח**: ויאמר אברהם אל האלקים, לו ישמעאל יחיה לפניך, ויאמר אלקים: אבל שרה אשתך יולדת בן, וקראת את שמו יצחק והקמותי את בריתי אתו, לברית עולם, לזרעו אחריו.

9 **שם יז, טו**: ויאמר אלקים אל אברהם, שרי אשתך, לא תקרא את שמה שרי, כי שרה שמה (פי׳ ת״ת — דכתי׳, כי שרה שמה בלשון שמובן בו העבר ולא בלשון עתיד והיה שמה שרה, כמו דכתי׳ באברהם).

10 **שם יז, ה**: ולא יקרא עוד את שמך אברם והיה שמך אברהם, כי אב המון גוים נתתיך.

11 "כי שרה שמה" (שם יז, טו) שרי היא שרה, בתחלת נעשית שרי לאומתה ולסוף נעשית שרה לכל העולם (ברכות יג.).

12 **בראשית כד, סז**: ויבאה יצחק האהלה שרה אמו, ויקח את רבקה ותהי לו לאשה ויאהבה וינחם יצחק אחרי אמו.

13 **שם כג, ב**: ויבא אברהם לספוד לשרה ולבכותה.

14 **שם כג, א**: ויהיו חיי שרה מאה שנה ועשרים שנה ושבע שנים שני חיי שרה — פי׳ רש״י — לכך נכתב שנה בכל כלל וכלל, לומר לך, שכל אחד נדרש לעצמו, בת ק׳ כבת כ׳ לחטא: מה בת כ׳ לא חטאה שהרי אינו בת עונשין, אף בת ק׳ בלא חטא. ובת כ׳ כבת ז׳ ליופי; "שני חיי שרה" — כולן שוין לטובה.

Chapter X

MAY WE INTERPRET ḤUKIM?

The laws of the Torah are usually classified in two categories, *mishpatim* and *ḥukim*. *Mishpatim* are commandments which presumably reflect humanistic considerations and are supported by our social conscience. *Ḥukim* are laws whose rationale is not apparent to us; and were it not for the Divine imperative, we would not perform them. Both are mandated by the Torah, "You shall do My laws [*mishpatim*] and keep My decrees [*ḥukim*], for I am God, your Lord" (Lev. 18:4; Yoma 67b).[1]

The most stupefying of the six *ḥukim* listed in the Talmud is the law of the *Parah Adumah* (Num. 19), which involves striking contradictions. "Though Satan [Rashi: the evil inclination, the *yetzer ha-ra*] and Gentiles taunt Israel," ridiculing its irrationality, our Sages admonished that "It is My decree and you have no right to question it" (ibid.). To probe the mystery of its effectiveness is both futile and frustrating. We accept it as an enigma which the human mind cannot unravel.

Nevertheless, Rashi recorded the commentary of R. Moshe Hadarshan (ibid., v. 22), who elaborately interprets all aspects of the *Parah Adumah,* the symbolic significance of the ingredients of the watery ashes and its remarkable effectiveness as a ritual cleanser. Other exegetes have done likewise. Since the Talmud discourages and seems to forbid such probing, why do scholars persist in such inquiry?

It is our thesis that one may distinguish between motivations, explanations, and interpretations. Ascribing Divine motivations is a hopeless exercise; explaining how the ritual achieves its purpose is a futile enterprise. But offering a subjective interpretation which will strengthen its spiritual meaning for the worshipper is not only permissible, but should even be encouraged. Maimonides extolled "those who have succeeded in finding proofs [understanding] for everything that can be explained" (Guide 3:51),[2] and Rabbenu Baḥya (eleventh-century Jewish philosopher and moralist) urged the use of intellect "so that your faith and practice may rest on foundations of tradition and reason" (Ḥovot Halevavot, Intro.).[3]

Three Types of Questions

There are three types of questions we may ask about any phenomenon. "Why" probes *motivations* to establish why things are the way they are; "how" seeks *explanations* as to how they function effectively; and "what" looks for *interpretations* to establish meaningfulness. "Why" and "how" pertain to qualities which presumably are inherent in things; "what" deals with subjective formulations which are superimposed by the beholder for purposes of utility and convenience.

In the exact sciences of physics and chemistry, we never ask "why" because that is a metaphysical, not a scientific, question. There can be no scientific "why" for water's freezing at 32 degrees Fahrenheit or for light's traveling at 186,000 miles per second. But "how" is a legitimate pursuit which searches for causal relationships of varied phenomena and seeks to define their interrelationships in mathematical terms. The answer to "how" makes control and predictability possible.

In contrast, botany and zoology are purely descriptive disciplines, classifying plants and animal life. They answer "what" by imposing categories and groupings upon otherwise disorganized data. Order is imposed on chaos. Classifications are subjective though not arbitrary. Their formulations are influenced by their utility to man. It is obviously more useful and convenient to deal with ten or twenty broad categories based on particular similarities than to cope intelligently with millions of varied

May We Interpret Ḥukim? / 93

data. If we venture to pose the question "how" in botany or zoology, we have abandoned these disciplines and have strayed into organic chemistry, which is concerned with functioning and effectiveness.

Asking "Why" for Mitzvot

Applying each of the above three questions regarding God and His *mitzvot,* one meets with differing results. Asking "why" God issued certain commandments is seeking to comprehend the unfathomable. It is more than simply a matter of being unable to comprehend God's mind and motivation. It is more profound than that. When we ask "why" in the human context, we are truly asking "what motivated Him?" A correct reply would be that in order to achieve objective B, agent A had to be employed, because otherwise B would remain inaccessible.

Obviously, one cannot reason in this manner about God, as though He had to overcome some inability or deficiency by using an intermediary agent. All is readily accessible and realizable to Him. The best and only answer to any question about God's motivations is "He willed it," *gezerah hi milfanei* (Guide 3:13).[4]

In response to the question "Why did God create the world?" we should not say that He is kind and wanted to bestow goodness on the world or that a king needs a kingdom. The very notion of need implies that He had an insufficiency which He sought to overcome. This is obviously untenable. The only acceptable answer is, "He willed it." That takes care of the matter—God's will is self-justifying. In the case of man, we cannot reply "he willed it," because man is not self-sufficient, and one may ask further, "but why did he will it, what did he lack which he sought to attain?"

Not being able to provide the "why" of *mitzvot* does not mean that there are no objective reasons for them. Naḥmanides (on Lev. 19:19) taught: "The intention of the Rabbis [in defining *ḥukim* as laws for which there is no reason] was not that these are Divine decrees for which there are no reasons whatever, for 'every word of God is purifying [refined]' [Prov. 30:5]. Rather, *ḥukim* are like enactments which a king promulgates without revealing their benefits to the people, who, not sensing their reasons, entertain questions about them in their hearts even as they comply nevertheless. Similarly, the *ḥukim* of the Holy One, blessed be He, are His secrets in the Torah which people, by means of their thinking, do not grasp as they do in the case of *mishpatim*, but yet they all have a proper reason and a perfect benefit."[5]

Maimonides agrees with this view: "There is cause for every commandment" (Guide 3:26).[6] The Midrash in Numbers Rabbah 19:4 declares that *Parah Adumah*, the most intractable of all *ḥukim*, is an enigma to us, but its rationale was divulged to Moses.[7] There are reasons for *ḥukim* which are unknown to us.

Asking "How" for Mitzvot

Asking "how" for *ḥukim* is also nonsensical. How does the sprinkling of the watery ashes of the *Parah Adumah* cleanse the ritually unclean (Num. 19)? How does the goat sent to Azazel bring forgiveness on Yom Kippur (Lev. 16)? How does *ḥalitzah* release a widow for remarriage (Deut. 28)? We willingly and reverently accept the incomprehensible "how" even as we dutifully embraced the unfathomable "why."

In contrast, asking "why" and "how" for *mishpatim* does seem to be legitimate and promising. We think we know the motivations for the prohibitions against stealing, murder, adultery, and false testimony and for the positive commandments which reflect a sensitivity to the rights and welfare of others. They seem morally uplifting and socially stabilizing. In fact, however, their moral reasonableness is often in question in our modern world. The campaigns to legitimize abortion, euthanasia, adultery, and homosexuality are examples of the unreliability of the social conscience even with *mishpatim*. Clearly, *mishpatim* too must be accepted as *ḥukim*, lest they be rationalized away.

Asking "What" for Mitzvot

Remaining is the third question, "what," which inquires about the meaningfulness of particular *mitzvot* to the individual and to society. This is a legitimate pursuit. Nay, it may even be meritorious to inquire, "How can I integrate and assimilate this *mitzvah* into my religious consciousness and outlook?" "What thoughts and emotions should I feel when the *Parah Adumah* chapter is read in the synagogue?" "How can it help me achieve *devekut*, a greater closeness to God?"

Such questions reflect the need to be intellectually and emotionally engaged in the performance of a *mitzvah*, even of *ḥukim*. One does not ask, "Why did God legislate *Parah Adumah*?" or "How does it purify the ritually defiled?" but "What is its spiritual message to me?" or "How can I, as a thinking and feeling person, assimilate it into my world outlook?" When we say the *Shema*, we experience an acceptance of Divine sovereignty but what should we feel when we scrupulously avoid admixtures of meat and dairy?

This is what R. Moshe Hadarshan, cited by Rashi, attempted to do—to suggest an interpretation which would heighten the meaningfulness of the *Parah Adumah* to us.

The Status of a "Servant of the Lord"

That an experience of a *mitzvah* in depth is highly preferred is supported by the Talmudic interpretation of a verse in Malachi 3:18. "And you shall come to see the difference between the righteous [*tzaddik*] and the wicked [*rasha*]; between him who is a servant of the Lord [*oved Elohim*] and him who is not a servant of the Lord [*lo avado*]."

The Talmad (Hag. 9b) asks: "Is not a *tzaddik* identical to an *oved Elohim;* is not a *rasha* the same as *lo avado?*" Are they not synonymous terms? The answer of the Talmud is that no parallelism is here intended between the first and second clauses.* While the first clause contrasts a *tzaddik* and a *rasha*, the second alludes to two types of *tzaddikim*, the *tzaddik oved Elohim* and the *tzaddik lo avado*.[8]

The Baal Hatanya, R. Shneur Zalman of Lyady, the founder of Ḥabad Ḥassidism (1747–1812), explains the distinction as follows: The *tzaddik oved Elohim* is emotionally and intellectually engaged in the *mitzvah*, which is evidenced by his readiness to go beyond minimal performance. He is continually conscious of a joyous privilege and will, therefore, regularly surpass himself. The *tzaddik lo avado* acts out of a habituated nature, though he is punctiliously observant. The emotional accompaniment is lacking, and additional initiatives are rarely forthcoming.

This is what the Talmud means when it states that the *lo avado* is content to review his Torah lessons one hundred times, a customary round figure, while the *oved Elohim* will review one hundred and one times, surpassing usual expectations (Likutei Amarim, chap. 15).[9]

Thus, every *mitzvah*, even a *ḥok*, should ideally engage us and communicate some personal message if we are to attain the status of *oved Elohim*. We have questioning minds, and even if "why" and "how" elude us, we should strive to rationalize the "what." It is one's mind and emotions which transform a physical act into a worshipful performance.

The Mitzvah of Shilu'aḥ Hakan

That we may rationalize a *mitzvah* in terms of its utility to man is supported by Naḥmanides' interpretation of the *mitzvah* of *Shilu'aḥ Hakan*. In Deuteronomy 22:6 we read: "If you come across a bird's nest on any tree or on the ground, and it contains

---

*A synonymous parallelism exists when the second clause repeats the ideas of the first clause in different words, e.g., "a fool's mouth is his ruin, and his lips are the snare of his mouth" (Prov. 18:7).

May We Interpret Ḥukim? / 97

baby birds or eggs, then, if the mother is sitting on the chicks or eggs, you must not take the mother along with her young. You must first chase away the mother, and only then may you take the young. [If you do this] you will have it good, and will live long."[10]

Maimonides ascribed Divine compassion for the mother bird as the motivation for the *mitzvah*, "since the suffering of animals under such circumstances . . . does not differ from that of man, since love and tenderness of the mother for the young is not produced by the intellect but by the emotions, and this faculty exists not only in man but in most living things" (Guide 3:48).[11]

Maimonides' view is contradicted by the Mishnah (Ber. 5:3): "One who says, 'Thy mercy extends to the bird's nest' is to be silenced."[12] This is understood as referring to a public reader, *sheli'aḥ tzibbur,* who in leading a formal prayer service says: "Just as You have compassion on the mother bird in the *mitzvah* of *Shilu'aḥ Hakan,* so be You compassionate with us." Such manner of formal prayer is not permitted because it is based on an assumption that compassion is the reason for the *mitzvah*. This cannot be accepted with certainty, and it is wrong to render a prayer in behalf of the community contingent on an uncertain hypothesis.*

Naḥamanides disagrees with Maimonides. He questions whether the ruling on the mother bird is based on the Almighty's pity for the animal. "Otherwise, He would have forbidden their slaughter. The reason, however, for the prohibition is to teach us compassion and the avoidance of cruelty. Professional animal killers often become hardened to human suffering by their occupation. Not to slaughter the mother and the young on the same day and sending away the mother bird . . . are decrees to inculcate humanity in us" (Deut. 22:6).[13] The Mishnah previously cited as troublesome to Maimonides is perfectly in accord with Naḥmanides' judgment. Not compassion, but pedagogy, is

---

*In private prayer or in sermonic interpretations of a text, such would not be prohibited.

involved. A *mitzvah* is to be interpreted in terms of *to'elet ba-adam*, its meaningfulness and usefulness to man.

Conclusion

Accepting *mitzvot*, even *ḥukim*, with pious obedience is meritorious, but ascribing an interpretative meaning, heightens the spiritual experience. Thereby may we achieve the exemplary status of *tzaddik oved Elohim*, engaging us both intellectually and emotionally in the worship of God.

הערות לפרק 10

1   **ויקרא יח, ד**: "את משפטי תעשו" — ת"ר דברים שאלמלא לא נכתבו, דין הוא שיכתבו, ואלו הן: עבודת כוכבים, וגלוי עריות, ושפיכת דמים, וגזל, וברכת השם; "את חקתי תשמרו" (שם), דברים שהשטן (רש"י — יצר הרע) משיב עליהן ואלו הן, אכילת חזיר, ולבישת שעטנז, וחליצת יבמה, וטהרת מצורע, ושעיר המשתלח. ושמא תאמר, מעשה תוהו הם, ת"ל, "אני ה'" — אני ה' חקקתיו ואין לך רשות להרהר בהן (יומא סז, ב).

2   **רמב"ם, מורה נבוכים ח"ב פנ"א**: אבל מי שהושגה לו ההוכחה על כל מה שהוכח, ונתברר לו מן העניינים האלקיים כל מה שאפשר לברר אותו, וקרב אל הנכון במה שאי אפשר בו אלא קירוב אל הנכון, כבר נמצא עם המלך בתוך החצר.

3   **רבנו בחיי, "חובות הלבבות" — הקדמה**: אם אתה איש דעת ותבונה, שתוכל לעמוד בהם על ברור מה שקבלת מהחכמים בשם הנביאים משרשי הדת וקוטבי המעשים, אתה מצווה להשתמש בהם עד שתעמוד על העניין ויתברר לך מדרך הקבלה והשכל יחד. ואל תתעלם ותפשע בדבר, תהיה כמקצר במה שאתה חייב לבוראך יתברך.

4   **רמב"ם, מורה נבוכים ח"ג פי"ג**: והכרתי הוא שיסתיים הדבר במתן התכלית, שכך רצה ה' או כך גזרה חכמתו, וזה הנכון, וכך תמצא חכמי ישראל תקנו בתפלותיהם, באמרם, אתה הבדלת אנוש מראש ותכירהו לעמוד לפניך, כי מי יאמר לך מה תעשה ואם יצדק מה יתן לך (בנוסח הודוי של תפלת נעילה), הנה בארו שאין שם תכלית אלא הרצון המוחלט (תרגום יוסף קאפח).

5   **רמב"ן, ויקרא יט, יט**: ואין הכונה בהם שתהיה גזרת מלך מלכי המלכים בשום מקום בלא טעם, כי "כל אמרת אלוקה צרופה" (משלי ל, ה), רק החוקים הם גזירת המלך אשר יחוק במלכותו בלי שיגלה תועלתם לעם. ואין העם נהנים בהם אבל מהרהרין אחריהם בלבם ומקבלים אותם ליראת המלכות. וכן חוקי הקב"ה הם הסודות אשר לו בתורה שאין העם במחשבתם נהנים בהם כמשפטים אבל כולם בטעם

נכון ותועלת שלימה.

6 **רמב"ם, מורה נבוכים ח"ג פכ"ו**: שהמצוות כולם יש להם סבה ומפני התועלת צווה בהם, והיות לכולם עלה אלא שאנחנו נסכל עלת קצתם ולא נדע אופני החכמה בהן, הוא דעתינו כולנו.

7 **במד"ר יט, ד**: א"ל הקב"ה למשה: לך אני מגלה טעם פרה אבל לאחר חוקה.

8 **חגיגה ט, ב**: מאי כתיב ושבחם וראיתם בין צדיק לרשע, בין עובד אלקים לאשר לא עבדו (מלאכי ג, יח). — היינו צדיק, היינו עובד אלקים; היינו רשע, היינו אשר לא עבדו. (פי' רש"י — מי הוא צדיק ומי הוא עובד אלקים, הלא אחד הוא). אמר לו: עבדו, ולא עבדו, תרוייהו צדיקי גמורים נינהו, ואינו דומה שונה פרקו מאה פעמים לשונה פרקו מאה ואחד (פי' רש"י — אע"פ ששניהם צדיקים, לא עבדוהו בשוה, שזה עבדו יותר).

9 **לקוטי אמרים תניא פט"ו**: ולכן, זאת הפעם המאה והאחת היתה על הרגילות שהורגל מנעוריו שקולה כנגד כולן ועולה על גביהן, ביתר שאת ויתר עז, להיות נקרא עובד אלקים, מפני שבכדי לשנות טבע הרגילות צריך לעורר את האהבה לה' ע"י שיתבונן בגדלות ה' במוחו לשלוט על הטבע.

10 **דברים כב, ו**: כי יקרא קן צפור לפניך בדרך בכל עץ או על הארץ, אפרוחים או ביצים, והאם רובצת על האפרוחים או על הביצים, לא תקח האם על הבנים, שלח תשלח את האם ואת הבנים תקח לך, למען ייטב לך, והארכת ימים.

11 **רמב"ם, מורה נבוכים ח"ג פמ"ח**: וכן נאסר לשחוט אותו ואת בנו ביום אחד, סיג והרחקה שמא ישחט מהם הבן לפני האם, כי צער בעלי חיים בכך גדול מאד, כי אין הבדל בין צער האדם ובכך וצער שאר בעלי חיים כי אהבת האם וחנינתה על הבן אינו תוצאה של ההגיון אלא פעולת הכח המדמה המצוי ברוב בעלי חיים כמציאותו באדם . . . וזהו הטעם גם בשלוח הקן (תרגום קאפח).

12 **ברכות (פ"ה, מ"ג)**: האומר על קן צפור יגיעו רחמיך — משתקין אותו. רמב"ם מו"נ ג, מח: ואל תקשה עלי באמרם חז"ל "האומר על קן צפור יגיעו רחמיך וכו'" — כי זו אחת משתי הסברות אשר הזכרונם כלומר השקפת מי שסובר שאין טעם למצות אלא הרצון המופשט, ואנו הלא הלכנו אחרי ההשקפה השניה.

13 **רמב"ן, דברים כב, ו**: שאין רחמיו מגיעין בבעלי הנפש הבהמות למנוע אותנו מלעשות בהם צרכינו, שאם כן היה אוסר השחיטה, אבל טעם המניעה ללמד אותנו מדת הרחמנות ושלא נתאכזר, כי האכזריות תתפשט בנפש האדם, כידוע בטבחים שוחטי השורים הגדולים והחמורים שהם אנשי דמים, זובחי אדם, אכזרים מאד . . . והנה המצות האלה בבהמה ובעוף אינן רחמנות עליהם אלא גזירות בנו להדריכנו וללמד אותנו המדות הטובות.

Chapter XI

INTERPRETING THE PARAH ADUMAH

The *mitzvot* of the Torah are intended to engage us emotionally and intellectually. Otherwise they are reduced to cold, mechanical performances, devoid of personal meaning. They become soulless experiences, when, in fact, they were intended "to purify the people therewith" (Gen. R. 44:1).[1] In the preceding chapter we established the premise that we are encouraged to interpret all *mitzvot,* even *ḥukim,* statutes, which are usually defined as incomprehensible and about which our Sages warned that we may be tempted "to dismiss them as meaningless" (Yoma 67b).[2] They can be interpreted in terms of their subjective meaningfulness to us even if their objective rationale eludes us.

Maimonides' Interpretation of Mikveh

That we may ascribe moral interpretations for *ḥukim* is illustrated in Maimonides' summary comments about immersion in a *mikveh*. He writes as follows:

"It is plain and obvious that the laws of uncleanness [*tumah*] and cleanness [*taharah*] are decrees laid down by Scripture [*gezerat hakatuv*] and not matters about which human understanding is capable of forming a judgment; for behold, they are included among the Divine statutes [*ḥukim*]. So, too, immersion [in a *mikveh*] as a means of freeing oneself from uncleanness is included among the Divine statutes. Now, 'uncleanness' is not mud or filth, which water can remove, but is a matter of Scriptural decree and is dependent on the intention of the heart.

Therefore, the Sages have said, if a man immerses himself but without intention, it is as if he had not immersed himself at all.

"Nevertheless, we find some suggestiveness [moral basis], for just as he who has the intention to become clean becomes clean as soon as he immerses himself, although nothing new had befallen his body, so, too, one who sets his heart on cleaning himself from the uncleanness that besets men's soul—namely, wrongful thoughts and false convictions—becomes clean as soon as he consents in his heart to shun these counsels and brings his soul in the waters of pure reason. Behold, Scripture says, 'And I will sprinkle clean water upon you and you shall be clean; from all your uncleanness and from all your idols I will clean you' [Ezek. 36:25]" (Hil. Mikva'ot 11:12).[3]

Maimonides is suggesting that even as we perform rituals in accordance with God's will, whose reasons are inscrutable, we may ascribe subjective interpretations in order to give meaning to our spiritual experience.

The Enigma of Parah Adumah

Our Sages singled out the *Parah Adumah* (Red Heifer, Num. 19) ritual as the most mystifying of all *ḥukim*. The Midrash records the comment of King Solomon: "I have mastered everything, but the explanation of the *Parah Adumah* has escaped my intensive investigation." This is implicit in the verse in Ecclesiastes 7:23, "I said I will achieve wisdom [of the *Parah Adumah*], but it eluded me" (Num. R. 19:14).[4] Despite the forewarnings of its enigmatic character, we intend to offer an interpretation of the ritual and, thereby, to establish its meaningfulness as a religious experience. Indeed, Rashi records the commentary of R. Moshe Hadarshan (Num. 19:22), who elaborately interprets all aspects of the *Parah Adumah,* and other exegetes have done likewise.

We generally assume that the *ḥukah* aspect of the ritual, its incomprehensibility, is in its manner of preparation, its strange effectiveness in removing ritual uncleanness, and the prescription that it be slaughtered outside the Temple grounds, *shehutei hutz,* which is strictly forbidden with other sacrifices (Lev. 17:3). A further paradox inheres in its contradictory effect of simultaneously cleansing the defiled even as it contaminates those who are handling the watery ashes, *metahor et hatemayim u'metaher et hatehorim.*[5] No wonder that heathens, in the days of R. Yohanan ben Zakkai (first century), accused the Jews of practicing sorcery through the *Parah Adumah.*[6]

Death as the Hukah

We propose that the singular *hukah* here is not merely in the performance of the ritual but rather in the mind-defying mystery of death itself, whose defiling effects the watery ashes seek to counter. Death, the Torah tells us, has a contaminating effect; contact with it disqualifies us from entering the Temple and from participating in other matters of holiness. Death is a mocking fate which awaits us all, a trauma of human helplessness which disturbs our existential serenity. It is an absurdity which undoes all of man's rational planning, his dreams and hopes. We wonder, why should the foremost of God's creations have an awareness of his mortality and, therefore, live in constant dread and distress in face of its inevitability?

The concept that death defiles is probably unique to our faith. Judaism never equated death with holiness. The Zohar writes: "Death deprives the Jew of his Creator's holiness, his Divine image [*tzelem Elohim*], and his holy spirit; what remains is the lowly body."[7] God is called *Elohim hayyim,* "Living God" (Deut. 5:23), and the Torah is described as *etz hayyim,* "a tree of life" (Prov. 3:18). In contrast, the Egyptian civilization from which the Israelites emerged was obsessed with death, and Egyptians were commonly engaged in lifelong preparation for the hereafter.[8]

In Judaism, the *kohen* (priest) is enjoined "not to defile himself for any [dead] person except for his closest kin" (Lev. 21:2), and the *kohen gadol* (High Priest) was restricted even from his closest dead relatives (ibid.:11). A Nazirite, who assumed religiously motivated vows of self-deprivation, was as severely restricted as regards contact with the dead as the *kohen gadol* (Num. 6:7). The only exception which suspended all restrictions was with a *met mitzvah,* a forsaken corpse, one without attendant family or friends, where everyone was duty-bound to participate in the burial. Finally, Jews, even non-*kohanim*, who were defiled by a corpse, had to cleanse themselves with the *Parah Adumah* waters before they were allowed to come in contact with anything appertaining to the Sanctuary or to engage in such rituals as the paschal lamb sacrifice (Num. 9:6).

That the real *ḥukah* is death is intimated by a similarity of phraseology in the text. The chapter which introduces the *Parah Adumah* opens with the words *Zot ḥukat hatorah,* "this is the statute of the law." What is this *ḥukah?* In verse 14, it is identified as *zot hatorah, adam ki yamut,* "this is the law, if a man dies." The *ḥukah* previously indicated is death itself, which is the ultimate mystery of human existence.

Different Types of Ritual Defilement

Ritual uncleanness should not be confused with hygienic uncleanness, though the two may, at times, coincide. One can be bodily immaculate and still be ritually defiled. Particular experiences specified by the Torah and amplified by our Sages cause one to become ritually contaminated, *tamei,* and, as a consequence, to be restricted from participation in matters of holiness, *davar shebekdusha*. Procedures of purification to restore one to a ritually clean state, *tahor,* are set forth by the Torah. These are immersion, *tevillah,* for all types of defilement, and sprinkling, *haza'ah,* which is additionally required for one defiled by a corpse, *tumat-met*. These will be explained.*

*Glossary of terms: *tumah*—that which is ritually unclean; *tumot*—plural form of *tumah;* *tamaei*—one who is defiled; *tahor*—one who is ritually clean; *tumat met*—defiled through contact with human corpse; *tevillah*—immersion, a restorative to ritual cleanness; *haza'ah* (sprinkling)—an additional restorative to ritual cleanliness for *tumat-met*.

All ritual defilements have one common denominator, namely, being exposed to experiences which are depressing, ugly, and life-negating, all of which are emotionally and aesthetically jarring: bodily secretions (Lev. 15—*zav, zavah*), diseases involving bodily erosion (Lev. 14—leprosy), decaying dead organisms (Lev. 11:24—*sheretz, nevelah*), a human corpse (Num. 19). These are the sources of ritual uncleanness. Experiences with terminated life and organic decomposition affect us adversely and generate unwholesome feelings which conflict with the life-affirming emphasis of holiness. Our Sages taught, "one may not worship in sadness [melancholia] . . . but only in rejoicing with the *mitzvah* [with an optimistic frame of mind]" (Ber. 31a).[9]

The Additional Dimension of Human Death

Tumat-met shares with other *tumot* the characteristic of dealing with a dead organism. But *tumat-met* involves something more horrible, namely, human death. Death is an unpleasant experience when encountered in the zoological kingdom, but it involves no more than the cessation of functioning of an organism. With *tumat-met*, however, a spiritual personality has been terminated, a self-conscious individuality who was possessed of visions, hopes, joys, despair, and grief, a being who anticipated the future, remembered the past, and shaped the present. We are dealing with a human personality who had the capacity to build and destroy worlds.

In a word, human death is a most tragic event. Man, endowed with time-awareness, knows that his existence is transient. Even as he relates to God, he knows that death will terminate his earthly worship. The Sages tell us that what most disturbed them about death was that it interrupted their service of God. When R. Judah Hanasi was gravely ill, R. Ḥiya came to visit him and found him weeping. Whereupon, R. Ḥiya said to him: "Why are you crying? Are we not taught that when one dies cheerfully, it is a good sign, but when one dies weeping, it is a bad omen" (suggesting an awareness of sinfulness). R. Judah replied: "I am weeping because of the Torah and the meritorious deeds which I shall no longer be able to perform" (Ket. 103b).[10] Whatever beneficent rewards awaited him in the hereafter, they did not compare to the privilege of Torah study and the performance of good deeds here on earth. Death is an enemy; it is destructive of holiness. The psalmist said: "The dead praise not the Lord, neither any that go down in silence; but we [the living] shall praise the Lord from this time forth and evermore" (Ps. 115:17–18).[11]

Death in the animal world is not tragic. The species is not diminished by the death of an individual. Among brutes, the individual's significance is only as a representative of a particular class. God's concern is with the preservation of the species. "In the subluminary portion of the universe, Divine Providence [compassionate concern] does not extend to individual members of the species, except in the case of man" (Maimonides, Guide 3:17). Man, however, does not live as a representative of his group but because of his own inherent individual worth. He has autonomous value.

Each person is a microcosm, an *olam katan,* an individuality with dignity, an original with worthiness. "A single man was created to proclaim the greatness of God, for man mints many coins with one die, and they are all like one another; but God has stamped every man with the die of Adam, yet not one of them is like his fellow" (Sanh. 38a). Man's singular humanity establishes his status, not the class or society of which he is part. Every person can say, not with arrogance but in a spirit of personal challenge, "it is for my sake that the world was created," *bishvili nivra ha-olam* (ibid.). Again, "only a single person was created to teach us that he who destroys one individual, Scripture imputes it to him as though he had caused the whole world to perish, and he who saves a single individual, it is as if he preserved an entire world" (ibid.).[12] That is why human death is so abhorrently ugly.

Tumet-met is an enemy ever lurking in the shadows which

disturbs our serenity precisely because we are conscious of its inexorable finality.

Two Types of Purification

We may infer that *tumat-met* is significantly different from other *tumot* from the fact that it is recorded in the Torah separately, in Numbers (chap. 19 [Parashat Ḥukat]), while all the other *tumot* are grouped together in Leviticus (11:24 [Parashat Shemini] and chaps. 12 and 15 [Parashat Tazria and Metzora]). Also, *tumat-met* is introduced in the text with a declaratory pronouncement, *Zot ḥukat hatorah,* "this is the statute of the Torah," suggesting that we are dealing with an ultimate *ḥukah,* of a different character and of greater severity which is deserving of special treatment. The *Parah Adumah* chapter could have very appropriately been inserted in any of the *sidrot* (sections) dealing with the Tabernacle in Exodus (Terumah or Tetzaveh) or Leviticus (Ẓav or Shemini), since the ritual was revealed to Moses on the day the Tabernacle was erected and was first offered the next day (Git. 60a; Rashi, Lev. 8:34).[13]

The most significant difference between *tumat-met* and other *tumot* is in the method of purification which the Torah prescribes. The former requires *haza'ah* (sprinkling the watery ashes of the *Parah Adumah*) as well as *tevillah* in a *mikveh* (immersion in a gathering of water in accordance with the specifications of the halakhah). Other *tumot,* however, are cleansed solely through *tevillah* and require no *haza'ah*.[14]

This distinction in purification is emphasized in the Torah: "He who touches the corpse of any human being shall be unclean for seven days; he shall be cleansed through *haza'ah* on the third day and the seventh day, and then shall be clean; but if he purifies himself not on the third and seventh days, he shall not be clean" (Num. 19:11).[15] Why was there a need to emphasize the negative "but if he purifies himself not"? Was not the positive statement sufficient, and is not the negative implicitly understood? The answer is that the Torah is warning us not to take the *haza'ah* requirement lightly, not to equate *tumat-met* with other defilements where *tevillah* alone suffices. For *tumat-met*, *tevillah* is indispensable, but it is not sufficient without *haza'ah*.

How They Differ

The two cleansing acts, *haza'ah* and *tevillah*, are strikingly dissimilar in the manner of their performance, and one may derive lessons from each. *Tevillah* requires that the defiled enter the water entirely on his own initiative, bowing his head, bending his knees, and submerging in a sea, river, lake, or any other *mikveh*. He then emerges a *tahor*, cleansed. Only he can do it; if he is lazy or fearful of water, his status cannot be changed. The defiled must perform the act himself; it cannot be done for him. He defiled himself and he must cleanse himself. *Tevillah*, therefore, implies a capacity to change one's condition. It is suggestive of all forms of human initiative, creativity, and freedom, the ability of man to transform his life, to raise himself because he has free will. Man can remain defiled if he so wishes, and be reconciled to the restrictions it imposes, simply by not going to the *mikveh*. Or, if cleansing is desired, he must muster the initiative and pull himself up; it is all up to him.

Haza'ah also involves water, but the situation is different. The *tamei* cannot sprinkle it upon himself; it must always be "and a clean person shall sprinkle it upon the unclean person" (Num. 19:19). He cannot liberate himself; he is dependent upon others; only a *tahor* can help him. His is a condition of dependency, and his own initiative is not enough. Both *tevillah* and *haza'ah* remove defilement and render one eligible to participate in the holiness of the Temple. In the former, it is self-liberation; in the latter, he must depend on others.

Why is *tevillah* not sufficient for *tumat-met* as it is for other *tumot*?

Aesthetic Ugliness and Existential Ugliness

Tumat-met represents existential ugliness. An awareness of one's mortality casts a melancholic cloud of gloom upon all of men's strivings. Kohelet wrote: "For that which befalls the soul of man befalls the beasts; as one does, so does the other. Yea, they have but one breath; so man has no permanence above the beasts; for all is vanity" (Eccles. 3:19).[16] Other forms of *tumot,* however, involve aesthetic, not existential, ugliness; they are reactions to sense experiences which are jarringly disturbing. Both are depressants and are incongruous with holiness.

Aesthetic ugliness can be washed away by the waters of *tevillah.* The putrifaction and decomposition that characterize most *tumot* are negative and upsetting, but immersion can be psychologically rejuvenating. One submerges from the visual world and rises as if reborn, changed in status and identity, a *beriyah ḥadashah. Tevillah,* which is required for converts to Judaism, also connotes a total transformation of identity. For aesthetic ugliness, *tevillah* seems the appropriate therapy; it is an emotional antidote to an emotional ailment. But what does one do with *tumat-met,* which is an experience that, besides its aesthetic effects, also represents the frustration of man's dignity and hopes? This is an intellectually perceived ugliness which is built into the human condition; it is more than a reaction to a disturbing emotional experience.

Aesthetic ugliness yields to a corrective aesthetic cleansing. Existential ugliness, however, which is due to an awareness of one's inexorable mortality, is not effaced so readily. *Tevillah,* becoming a new person, does not remove this dread; death continues to frighten. How, then, can we come to terms with our morbid forebodings and overcome its life-negating effects? An additional method, *haza'ah,* besides the palliative *tevillah,* is needed.

The real cleanser of the morbid state induced by threatening death is God Himself. We have faith that He compassionately cares about us and that we will not be abandoned. We accept, both intellectually and emotionally, a sense of surety that the human soul, the real "I" in the human personality, is immortal, and that death is a transition, not a termination. These considerations assuage the terrors of death; it is no longer nihilistically destructive.

Eschatologically (*b'aḥrit ha-yamim,* in the end of days), we are assured by the prophet that God will conquer and undo death, nullifying its power to inflict anguish. "He will destroy death forever; and the Lord shall wipe away tears from all faces" (Isa. 25:8).[17] We confront death directly and deflate it of its terror. As the psalmist said: "Into Thy hand I commend my spirit; Thou hast redeemed me, O Lord God of truth" (Ps. 31:6).[18]

The ultimate purifier, *metaher,* from the defilement of *tumat-met* is God Himself. Our Sages clearly suggest that only He can lift from us the debilitating effects of contact with human death. On the verse "And one who is clean will gather up the ashes" (Num. 19:9), *v'asaf ish tahor,* the Tanchuma (B.) adds: "This refers to the Holy One." Verses are cited to support this interpretation.[19] It is the Almighty, represented by the *Tahor,* who is the ultimate purifier of the scourge and terror of death. The totally irrational ritual of the *Parah Adumah* suggests that human efforts to comprehend death and to lessen its dread are futile without an acceptance of a providential God. The inexorability of death as a human condition comes from Him, and only He can cleanse us. We cannot achieve it by ourselves.

Why Both Tevillah and Haza'ah?

We may now appreciate that *haza'ah* is necessary for *tumat-met.* Why, however, is *tevillah* also required for *tumat met?* Why is not *haza'ah* sufficient? The answer is that, in addition to our faith in God as the ultimate conqueror of death, we ourselves must also be engaged in the day-to-day struggle with death, to deflate its boldness and aggressiveness. *Tevillah,* which connotes human initiative, should also be employed to reduce the incidence of death, to relieve pain and its debilitating effects. To prolong life and to enhance its quality are dignified and noble endeavors. The Torah supports scientific research in the healing arts and sanctions the physician's role. On the verse, "And shall cause him to be thoroughly healed," *v'rapo yerapei* (Ex. 21:19), our Sages add: "This teaches us that authorization was granted by God to the physician to heal" (B. Kam. 85a).[20] Maimonides ruled that healing the sick is not only permissible but mandatory.[21] The Shulḥan Arukh adds: "He who withholds his services, it is considered as if he were shedding blood."[22] Also, "if a physician advises that an ill person eat on Yom Kippur, he is to be obeyed even if the patient wishes otherwise" (Yoma 83a).[23] Clearly, sickness and death are not to be accepted with complacency as Divine decrees, but are to be resisted on the premise that the Creator wishes us to utilize all resources to preserve life and health.

We cannot defeat death, but we can alleviate its effects upon us, both medically and psychologically, to limit its frequency and terror. Longevity can be extended through human initiative, as symbolized by *tevillah*. Earthly immortality, however, will continue to elude us, and only with God's help can we cleanse ourselves of mordibity and go on with our life's work. This is the symbolic message of *haza'ah*. *Tumat-met*, therefore, requires a double procedure of purification. The ultimate enigma, *Zot ḥukat hatorah*, is *adam ki yamut*, man's mortality.

Why is Parah Adumah in Sidrah Ḥukat?

We are guided by the principle of Naḥmanides that there is an *aḥdut ha-Torah*, a chronological unfolding of themes in the Torah, and that there is a logical continuity in the sequence of narratives. He writes: "I have insistently maintained that the Torah is faithful to chronology except where the text specifically states otherwise, and even then, when it is dictated by contextual and ideological needs" (Num. 16:1).[24]

Why, then, is the chapter of *Parah Adumah* situated in Ḥukat (Num. 19), surrounded by seemingly unrelated subjects? We have already explained that it is not grouped with the other *tumot* in Shemini, Tazria, and Metzora (all in Leviticus) in order to emphasize that *tumat-met* is of a separate rank of severity whose *taharah* requires *haza'ah* in addition to the usual *tevillah*. But the question persists: what is it doing in Ḥukat?

The Thirty-Year Blackout

The chapter of *Parah Adumah* is a bridge spanning events that happened thirty-eight years apart, from the rebellion of Korah (chaps. 16–18) to the arrival at the wilderness of Zin (chap. 20). It is a somber reflection of those tragic years during which the exodus generation, *Yotzei Mitzrayim,* was dying in the desert, making way for the generation of the desert, *dor hamidbar,* who were to enter the Holy Land. To represent the tragic death of an entire generation, the *Parah Adumah* chapter, with its message of triumph over the melancholy of death, is appropriately situated.

The logical transition of chapters may be explained as follows:

1. *Sidrah Shelaḥ* (chap. 14). The sin of the *meraglim* (spies) and the hysterical despair of the exodus generation, brought on the Divine decree that "you shall bear your punishment for forty years, corresponding to the number of days, forty days, that you scouted the land; a year for each day . . . in this wilderness they shall die to the last man."[25] The Midrash describes the deaths which occurred annually on Tisha B'Av, the anniversary of their loss of faith in reaction to the negative reports of the *meraglim*.[26] Our Sages noted that their profuse weeping that night was without justification. Had they not left Egypt and crossed the Red Sea miraculously! And were they not fed each day with manna! And had they not experienced the awesome Revelation at Sinai, where God spoke to them directly! Such despair was unwarranted. It testified to a scarred and slavish mentality which rendered them unworthy and physically incapable of conquering the land (Maimonides, Guide 3:24).

2. *Korah's Rebellion*. According to Naḥmanides, the Korah

rebellion followed the *meraglim* episode. "After sinning [in the matter of] the spies, Moses did not pray on their behalf, so that the decree against them was not annulled. The princes of all the tribes died by the plague before the Eternal, and it was decreed that the whole people would be consumed in the wilderness and that they should die. The mood of the whole people became embittered, and they said in their hearts that mishaps had occurred to them through Moses' words. Therefore, Korah found it an opportune occasion to contest Moses' deeds, thinking that the people would readily listen to him."[27]

All commentators agree that Korah's rebellion took place in the second year of the exodus. For the following thirty-eight years, a period of *hester panim* prevailed, God turning His face, so to speak, from His people. They retreated, they moved aimlessly in circular motion, without destination. It was a long, silent night without "affectionate, face-to-face" Divine communication between God and Moses (Rashi, Taanit 30; Deut. 2:17).[28] No new *mitzvot* were legislated. The sun had set for thirty-eight years when the dialogue was resumed and the painful vigil came to an end.

3. *Two Reassurances.* In Shelaḥ, after the Israelites are told they will expire in the desert, the Torah introduces the *mitzvah* of *ḥallah* (Num. 15:18), which is to be observed "when you enter the land to which I am taking you and you will eat of the bread of the land."[29] Similarly, at the end of Korah, we read of the emoluments of *terumah* and *ma'aser* (tithes), which are to be given to the *kohen* and *levi* "from the produce of the land" (18:8).[30] Rashi and Naḥmanides indicate that these commandments were communicated at this time to assure the people that no matter how long the delay, their children would surely inherit the Holy Land, where they would enjoy the produce and these *mitzvot* would then apply.[31] Precisely at this point of depression, they needed the reassurance that the Divine promise to the Patriarchs would eventually be fulfilled and the children of Israel would inhabit the land.

4. *Parah Adumah* (Num. 19). The painful period when an

entire generation died is, like the *Parah Adumah* ritual itself, a *hukah*, a Divine decree beyond human comprehension. The symbol of this mournful period is the *Parah Adumah*, which removes defilements derived from human death. It represents a triumph over death, an affirmation of life, and qualifies one to resume participation in matters of *kedushah*. As explained earlier, God is the ultimate purifier (*metaher*) who helps us overcome the depression of morbidity. *Parah Adumah* is an appropriate transition between the period of rejection and death, and the resumption of Divine communication when they arrived in Midbar Zin, in the fortieth year of their wanderings.

"And the children of Israel, even the whole congregation, *kal ha'edah*, arrived in the wilderness of Zin, in the first month, and the people stayed at Kadesh, and Miriam died and was buried there."[32] Rashi explains: "[*Kal ha'edah*] signifies that those who were to die in the desert had all expired, and that these, the new generation raised in the desert, *dor hamidbar*, were to live."[33]

From Korah's rebellion (16–19) to Midbar Zin there elapsed a period of thirty-eight years, and the *Parah Adumah* is an appropriate transition.

הערה לפרק 11

1   **ב"ר מד, א**: רב אמר לא נתנו המצוות אלא לצרף בהן את הבריות.

2   **יומא סז, ב**: שמא תאמר מעשה תוהו הוא, ת"ל "אני ה'" (ויקרא יח, ד), אני ה' גזרתיו ואין לך רשות להרהר בהן (רש"י, במדבר יט, ב ד"ה זאת חקת התורה).

3   **רמב"ם, הל' מקואות פי"א הי"ב**: דבר ברור וגלוי שהטומאות והטהרות גזירות הכתוב הן, ואינן מדברים שדעתו של אדם מכרעתו והרי הן מכלל החוקים, וכן הטבילה מן הטומאות מכלל החוקים היא שאין הטומאה טיט או צואה שתעבור במים אלא גזירת הכתוב היא, והדבר תלוי בכוונות הלב, ולפיכך אמרו חכמים טבל ולא הוחזק כאילו לא טבל, ואעפ"כ, רמז יש בדבר, כשם שהמכוין לבו לטהר, כיון שטבל טהור, ואע"פ שלא נתחדש בגופו דבר, כך המכוין לבו לטהר נפשו מטומאות הנפשות שהן מחשבות האון ודעות הרעות, כיון שהסכים בלבו לפרוש מאותן העצות והביא נפשו במי הדעת טהור, הרי הוא

אומר: "וזרקתי עליכם מים טהורים וטהרתם מכל טומאותיכם ומכל גלוליכם אטהר אתכם" (יחזקאל לו, כה).

4 **במדב"ר יט, ג**: אמר שלמה: על כל אלה עמדתי ופרשת פרה אדומה חקרתי ושאלתי ופשפשתי, "אמרתי אחכמה והיא רחוקה ממני" (קהלת ז, כג).

5 **רמב"ן, במדבר יט**: מה טעם לאומות שיהיו מונין אותנו בזאת יותר משאר הקרבנות שיכפרו, ויש מהם שיטהרו כקרבנות הזב והיולדת, כי מפני היותה נעשית בחוץ, יראה להם שהיא נזבחת לשעירים על פני השדה, פי' ספרנו — ומעיקרי ההעלם בזה (לשלמה) הוא שהיא מטמאה את הטהורים ומטהרת את הטמאים.

6 **במדב"ר יט, ד**: שאל גוי אחד את ר' יוחנן בן זכאי: אילין עובדייא דאתון עבדין (אלו מעשים שאתם עושים), נראין כמין כשפים.

7 **זהר**: ישראל בשעתא דאיהו מית, כל קדושי דמארי מתעברן מניה, אתעבר מניה האי צולמא קדישא ואתעבר מניה האי רוח קודשא אשתאר גופא מסאבא.

8 Edith Hamilton, "The Great Way to Western Civilization" (Mentor, 1942, p. 13).

9 **ברכות לא, א**: אין עומדים להתפלל לא מתוך עצבות... אלא מתוך שמחה של מצוה.

10 **כתובות קג, ב**: כשחלה רבי, נכנס ר' חייא אצלו ומצאו שהוא בוכה, א"ל, רבי, מפני מה אתה בוכה? והתניא, מת מתוך השחוק, סימן יפה לו, מתוך הבכי (מפני יראת מיתה), סימן רע לו. א"ל, אנא אתורה ומצוות בכינא (שיתבטלו ממנו).

11 **תהלים קטו, יז-יח**: לא המתים יהללו י-ה, ולא כל יורדי דומה, ואנחנו נברך י-ה, מעתה ועד עולם הללוי'.

12 **סנהדרין לז, א**: לפיכך נברא האדם יחידי, ללמדך, שכל המאבד נפש אחת מישראל מעלה עליו הכתוב כאלו איבד עולם מלא, וכל המקיים נפש אחת מישראל מעלה עליו הכתוב כאלו קיים עולם מלא... ולהגיד גדולתו של הקב"ה, שאדם טובע כמה מטבעות בחותם אחד, כולם דומין זה לזה ומלך מלכי המלכים הקב"ה טבע כל אדם בחותמו של אדם הראשון ואין אחד מהם דומה לחברו, לפיכך כל אחד ואחד חייב לומר, בשבילי נברא העולם.

13 **גיטין ס, א**: דאמר רבי לוי: שמונה פרשיות נאמרו ביום שהוקם בו המשכן... ופרשת פרה אדומה, פי' רש"י — לפי שביום המחרת נשרפה הפרה להיות נטהרין לפסחיהם... והכי אמרינן במסכת מגילה ירושלמי, באחד בניסן הוקם המשכן ושני לו נשרפה הפרה (ראה רש"י, ויקרא ח, לד ד"ה לעשות").

14 **במדבר יט, יג** — כל הנוגע במת בנפש האדם אשר ימות — פי' רש"י — ואי זה מת? של נפש האדם, להוציא נפש בהמה שאין טומאתה צריכה הזאת.

Interpreting the Parah Adumah / 115

15 **במדבר יט, יא**: הנוגע במת לכל נפש אדם וטמא שבעת ימים, הוא יתחטא בו ביום השלישי וביום השביעי יטהר, ואם לא יתחטא ביום השלישי וביום השביעי לא יטהר.

16 **קהלת ג, יט**: כי מקרה בני האדם ומקרה הבהמה ומקרה אחד להם, כמות זה כן מות זה ורוח אחד לכל ומותר האדם מן הבהמה אין כי הכל הבל.

17 **ישעי' כה, ח**: בלע המות לנצח, ומחה ה' אלקים דמעה מעל כל פנים.

18 **תהלים לא, ו**: בידך אפקיד רוחי פדיתה אותי ה' אל אמת.

19 **תנחומא (בובר, חקת ס, ב)**: ואסף — זה הקב"ה דכתיב "ונשא נס לגוים ואסף נדחי ישראל" (ישעי' יא, יב); "איש" — זה הקב"ה דכתיב בו "ה' איש מלחמה" (שמות טו, ג).

20 **ב"ק פה, א**: ורפא ירפא (שמות כא, יט) מכאן שנתנה רשות לרופא לרפאות (פי' שלא יאמר הרופא שסותר גזירת המלך).

21 **רמב"ם, פי' למשניות, נדרים פ"ד**.

22 **שו"ע יו"ד סי' של"ו ס"א**: ומצוה היא ובכלל פיקוח נפש הוא ואם מונע עצמו הרי זה שופך דמים.

23 **יומא פג, א**: רופא אומר צריך וחולה אומר אינו צריך, שומעין לרופא.

24 **רמב"ן, במדבר טז, א**: וכבר כתבתי, כי על דעתי, כל התורה כסדר, זולתי במקום אשר יפרש הכתוב ההקדמה והאחור, וגם שם ענין לטעם נכון.

25 **במדבר יד, לד-לה**: במספר הימים אשר תרתם את הארץ, ארבעים יום, יום לשנה, יום לשנה, תשאו את עונותיכם ארבעים שנה וידעתם את תנואתי . . . במדבר הזה יתמו ושם ימותו.

26 **תענית כט, א**: ויבכו העם בלילה ההוא (במדבר יד, א) אמר רבה א"ר יוחנן: אותו הלילה ליל תשעה באב היה (דמדייק הלשון "בלילה ההוא" דמשמע הלילה הידוע מקורות הימים הבאים), אמר להם הקב"ה, אתם בכיתם בכיה של חנם ואני קובע לכם בכיה לדורות.

27 **רמב"ן, במדבר טז, א**: וכאשר חטאו במרגלים, לא התפלל משה עליהם ולא בטלה הגזרה מהם, ומתו נשיאי כל השבטים במגפה לפני ה' ונגזר על כל העם שיתמו במדבר ושם ימותו, אז היתה נפש כל העם מרה והיו אומרים בלבם כי יבואו להם בדברי משה תקלות ואז מצא קרח מקום לחלוק על מעשיו וחשב כי ישמעו אליו העם.

28 **רש"י, דברים ב, יז**: "וידבר ה' אלי לאמר": אבל משלוח המרגלים עד כאן, לא נאמר בפרשה זו "וידבר" אלא "ויאמר" ללמדך שכל ל"ח שנה שהיו ישראל נזופים לא נתייחד עמו הדבור בלשון חבה פנים אל פנים וישוב הדעת, ללמדך שאין השכינה שורה על הנביאים אלא בשביל ישראל.

29 **במדבר טו, יח-כו**: בבואכם אל הארץ אשר אני מביא אתכם שמה, והיה באכלכם מלחם הארץ, תרימו תרומה לה', ראשית עריסותיכם,

חלה תרימו תרומה כתרומת גורן, כן תרימו אותה, מראשית עריסותיכם תתנו לה' תרומה לדורותיכם.

30 **שם יח, ח-כא:** וידבר ה' אל אהרן, ואני הנה נתתי לך את משמרת תרומתי לכל קדשי בני ישראל, לך נתתים למשחה ולבניך לחק עולם . . . כל חלב יצהר וכל חלב תירוש ודגן . . . בכורי כל אשר בארצם . . . כל תרומות הקדשים אשר ירימו בני ישראל לה' נתתי לך . . . ולבני לוי הנה נתתי כל מעשר בישראל לנחלה.

31 **רש"י, שם טו, ב:** כי תבואו — בשר להם שיכנסו לארץ; רמב"ן — ואולי היה זה עתה לנחמם ולהבטיחם, כי היו נואשים לומר, מי יודע מה יהיה לאורך ימים לסוף ארבעים שנה ואם יחטאו גם הבנים . . . הבטיחם שגלוי לפניו שיבואו ויירשו אותה.

32 **שם כ, א:** ויבואו בני ישראל כל העדה מדבר צין בחדש הראשון וישב העם בקדש ותמת שם מרים ותקבר שם.

33 **שם, רש"י:** כל העדה — עדה השלמה, שכבר מתו מתי מדבר ואלו פרשו לחיים (ראה רש"י, דברים ד, ד).

Chapter XII

FROM NEGATION TO AFFIRMATION

There are two distinct phases in the process of mourning. The Halakhah has meticulously insisted on their strict separation. The first period begins with the death of a relative for whom one is obligated to mourn and ends with burial. The second commences with burial and lasts seven or, in some respects, thirty days, and for parents, twelve months. The first we call *aninut;*[1] the second, *avelut.*[2] What is the halakhic and experiential distinction between these two phases of mourning?

Aninut, Self-Negation

Aninut (lit., trouble or sorrow; cf. Gen. 35:18, "Ben-oni") represents the spontaneous human reaction to death. It is an outcry, a howl of horror. Man responds to his defeat at the hands of death with total resignation and black despair. Beaten by the fiend, his prayers rejected, forsaken and lonely, man begins to question his singular worth. Doubt develops into cruel conviction, and doubting man turns into mocking man.

Whom does man mock? Himself! He downgrades and dehumanizes himself. He concludes that man is not human, that he is just an animal creature like the beast of the field. In a word, man's initial reaction to death is saturated with self-deprecation. If death is the final destiny of all men, if everything human terminates in the narrow confines of the grave, why make the pretense of being the choicest of all creatures? Why lay claim to singularity, and why pretentiously seek to imitate God's ways, *imitatio dei?* Why be committed? Why carry the human-moral load? Are we not just a band of conceited creatures who have somehow managed to delude ourselves of an imaginary superiority over the rest of creation? Wherein is the distinction of being in "God's image" if brute death can trample indiscriminately?

The Halakhah has displayed great compassion for perplexed, suffering man, firmly held in the clutches of his archenemy, death. It has never tried to gloss over the sorrowful, depressing spectacle of dying man. In spite of the fact that the Halakhah has indomitable faith in eternal life, in immortality, and in a continued transcendental existence for all human beings, it did understand, like a loving mother, man's fright and confusion when confronted with death. Therefore, the Halakhah has tolerated the *onen*'s torturing thoughts and doubts. It did not command him to disown them because they contradict the basic halakhic doctrine of man's election as the apex of creation. It permitted the *onen* to have his way for a while and has ruled that he be relieved of all positive *mitzvot*.

"One whose dead [relative] lies before him is exempt from the recital of the *Shema* and from prayer and from *tefillin* and from all precepts laid down in the Torah" (Ber. 17b).[3] The Yerushalmi, quoted by Tosafot, derives this law from a verse in Deuteronomy 16:3: [The Festival of Passover was commanded] "so that you remember the day of your departure from the land of Egypt as long as you live." To which our Sages append: "The commitment upon leaving Egypt was accepted as applicable to one preoccupied with life and not one who is involved with death."[4] (Rashi provides another explanation.)[5]

What is the reason behind this law exempting the mourner from the performance of *mitzvot?* Our commitment to God is rooted in our awareness of human dignity, *tzelem Elohim,* and sanctity. Once the perplexed, despairing individual begins to question whether or not such distinctiveness or specialness exists, the whole commitment is suspended. Man who has faith in himself, who is aware of his human charisma, was chosen to carry obligations and commandments. Despairing, skeptical, denying man was not so elected. How can man pray and address God if he doubts his very humanity, if speech is stripped by his doubts of its human characteristics and turned into mere physical sounds? How can the mourner pronounce a benediction or say "Amen" if he is speechless? He is still capable of producing sounds, but a benediction consists of spiritual words and not merely auditory words.

In a word, the motto of *aninut* is to be found in the morally pessimistic verse of Ecclesiastes: "For that which befalls the sons of man befalls the beast; both have the same end; as one dies so does the other; yes, they have the same breath; so that man has no preeminence above the beast; for all is vanity" (3:19).[6]

Avelut, Self-Affirmation

At this point, the halakhah makes an about-face. It is firmly convinced that man is free and that he is master not only over his deeds, but over his emotions as well. Man's control of his emotional life is unqualified, and he is capable of changing thought patterns and emotional moods within an infinitesimal period of time. He does not have to wait patiently for one mood to pass and for another to emerge gradually. He can disengage himself quickly and, in a wink, replace a disjunctive frame of mind with a redemptive one. Hence, the Halakhah, which showed so much tolerance for the mourner during the period of *aninut* and let him float with the tide of despair, now forcefully and with a shift of emphasis commands him that, with interment, *setimat hagolel,* the first phase of grief should come to a close and a second phase, that of *avelut,* begin.

The Ability to Switch Moods

The halakhic confidence that man can switch moods is illustrated in the law that a festival suspends the mourning period for the deceased. If one has begun his *shivah,* even a short time before the holiday started, the latter cancels the *shivah. Avelut* is more than an external ritual; it is an inner experience of pain which often strains one's faith. Similarly, *simḥat yom tov* includes not only ceremonial actions, but a genuine experience of joy as well. These two moods clash within the mourner, who finds his home bereft of his beloved and every corner full of memories.

Yet the halakhah commands: "Rise up from your mourning, cast the ashes from your head, change your clothes, light the festival lights, recite over a cup of wine the Kiddush extolling the Lord for giving us festivals of gladness, *mo'adim l'simḥah,* and sacred seasons of joy, pronounce the blessing *Sheheḥiyanu,* 'Blessed art Thou . . . who has kept us in life and has preserved and enabled us to reach this season,' join the jubilating community and celebrate the holiday as if nothing had transpired, as if the beloved person over whose death you grieve were still with you."

The halakhah, which at times can be very tender and accommodating, here acts as a disciplinarian demanding obedience, to cast off grief and to embrace joy. This metamorphosis, this leap from desolation to joy and trust, is an heroic gesture which we witness again and again amongst Torah-committed Jews. It is performed quietly, undemonstratively, in the dark night of loneliness.

Restoring One's Humanity

The mourner is now directed to undertake an heroic task, to start picking up the debris of his shattered personality and reestablish himself as a man, restoring his lost glory, dignity, and uniqueness. Instead of repeating to himself that man has no preeminence above the beast and that all is vanity, he is suddenly told by the halakhah to be mindful of the antithesis: "Thou hast distinguished man from the very beginning, and Thou hast considered him worthy of communicating with Thee" (lit., "of standing before Thee").[7] In the Yom Kippur *Ne'ilah,* this affirmation of man's cosmic worthiness follows his denigration in the earlier Ecclesiastes verse.

Yes, the Halakhah tells man that death is indeed ugly and frightening; yes, death trails every man, trying to defeat him, his ambitions and aspirations; all that is true. Our existence is exposed for its fragility, and the impact of our lives is shown for its transiency. Nevertheless, death must not plunge us into morbidity and immobility. We must not succumb to melancholic despair and self-pity. On the contrary, death challenges man to transcend his self-concern and anguish, to display greatness and to act heroically; to build even though he knows that he will not necessarily live to enjoy the sight of the magnificent edifice; to plant even though he may not eat of its fruits; to explore, to develop, to enrich, not for himself but for coming generations. There is work to be done within the family and for the *klal,* the larger community. The religious Jew, in particular, transcends his physical self by associating his life with the timeless covenantal destiny of the Torah community. Life assumes an enduring value, however curtailed be our years, through our participation in the perpetuation of the age-old *Mesorah.*

The Individual and the Community

The individual is mortal, but *Knesset Yisrael,* the Jewish community, is enduring. The halakhic principle of *ein tzibbur metim,* "the community does not die" (Tem. 15b) is rooted in the concept that the existence of *Knesset Yisrael* as a metaphysical unity surpasses the physical existence of its individual members. The individual is singularly important. Indeed, the sensitive halakhic rules of *avelut* are rooted in the Torah perception of each individual as a little world, a microcosm.[8] The death of an individual means that the communal spectrum has lost an irreplaceable special color. The saying "whoever saves one life in Israel, it is as if he had saved the entire world" (Sanh. 4:5) should be understood in this way. This being the case, death would be inconsolable with its crushing finality.

The Torah, however, also grants reality to the Jewish community, which is more than just an aggregate, an assembly of the many. Rather, it is a metaphysical entity, an individuality and not just a conglomerate. There is a personalistic identity and unity attached to the Jewish community. For example, Eretz Yisrael was not granted to individuals, but to *Knesset Yisrael*. Abraham did not receive the land as an individual, but as the father of a future nation. The owner of the Promised Land is *Knesset Yisrael*, which is a community persona. However strange such a concept may appear to empirical sociologists, it is not at all a strange experience for the halakhist and the mystic, to whom *Knesset Yisrael* is a living, loving, and compassionate mother.

Death curtails human life, but our input, our unique emphasis and influence, our dreams and hopes, continue towards realization through *Knesset Yisrael*. The prayer of *Niḥum Avelim*, consoling the mourners, *Hamakon yenaḥem*, "may the Almighty comfort you among the mourners of Zion and Jerusalem," calls upon the bereaved to identify with the travails of the larger community, to feel its pain, and be comforted by our faith in the future redemption.

Thus, not only does the realization of his mortality not free man from his commitment but, on the contrary, it enhances his role as an historic being and sensitizes his moral consciousness. Life is a challenge and an opportunity. "The day is short, the laborers are lazy, the reward is ample, the Master is strict and demanding" (Av. 2:4).[9]

While before burial, in *aninut*, man mourned in confusion and his grief expressed itself in an act of resignation from his greatness and choiceness, after burial man mourns in enlightened grief, in a heightened awareness of human greatness and election.

The Kaddish

The ceremonial turning point at which *aninut* is transformed into *avelut,* despair into intelligent sadness, self-negation into self-affirmation, is to be found in the *Kaddish* at the interment, *setimat hagolel.*

The *Kaddish* marks the beginning of a new phase of courageous and heroic mourning with a message of Divine salvation. What is the relationship between the proclamation of the solemn doxology, a hymn of praise of God, and burial? Through the *Kaddish* we hurl defiance at death and its fiendish conspiracy against man. When the mourner recites *Yitgadal v'yitkadash shemeh rabba,* "glorified and sanctified be Thy great Name," he declares more or less the following: No matter how powerful death is, notwithstanding the ugly end of man, however terrifying the grave is, however nonsensical and absurd everything appears, no matter how bleak one's despair is, we declare and profess publicly and solemnly that we are not giving up, that we are not surrendering, that we will carry on the work of our ancestors, that we will not be satisfied with less than the full realization of the ultimate goal—the establishment of God's kingdom, resurrection of the dead, and eternal life for man.

הערות לפרק 12

1 בראשית לה, יח: ותקרא שמו בן־אוני — פי׳ רש״י — בן צערי: "לא אכלתי באוני ממנו" (דברים כו, יד) — פי׳ רש״י — מכאן שאסור לאונן.

2 ירושלמי מו״ק פ״ג: מנין לאבל מן התורה שבעה, "ויעש לאביו אבל שבעת ימים" (בראשית נ, י). (אין הכונה שהיא מ״ע מה״ת אלא מסופר מה שנהגו ביעקב אבינו).

3 ברכות יז, ב: מי שמתו מוטל לפניו פטור מק״ש ומן התפלה ומן התפילין ומכל מצות האמורות בתורה (ודוקא מצות עשה הוא פטור אבל בלאוין בין של תורה ובין של דבריהם הוא חייב).

4 שם, תוס׳ ד״ה פטור מק״ש: בירושלמי מפרש טעמא. א״ר בון: כתיב "למען תזכור את יום צאתך מארץ מצרים כל ימי חייך" (דברים טז, ג) — ימים שאתה עוסק בחיים ולא ימים שאתה עוסק במתים (ומכאן למי שמתו מוטל לפניו פטור מק״ש ומתפילין והוא הדין בכל המצות).

5 רש״י, ברכות יז, ב: לפי שהוא טרוד במחשבת קבורתו והויא דומה דחתן דפטור משום טירדא דמצוה (הטעם, לפי שעוסק במצוה פטור מן המצה — סוכה כה, א).

6 **קהלת ג, יט**: כי מקרה בני האדם ומקרה הבהמה ומקרה אחד להם, כמות זה, כן כמות זה, ורוח אחד לכל, ומותר האדם מן הבהמה אין כי הכל הבל.

7 אתה הבדלת אנוש מראש, ותכירהו לעמוד לפניך (נעילה).

8 **רמב״ם, מורה נבוכים א, עב.**

9 **אבות פ״ב מ״כ**: רבי טרפון אומר: היום קצר והמלאכה מרובה, והפועלים עצלים והשכר הרבה ובעל הבית דוחק.

Chapter XIII

SITTING SHIVAH IS DOING TESHUVAH

The observance of *shivah, sheloshim,* and *yud beit ḥodesh* (for parents) is not only a catharsis of sorrow, but also an experience of self-judgment and penitence. *Avelut* is intrinsically an expression of *teshuvah*. The aching heart is a contrite heart, and a contrite heart seeks atonement. Enlightened and sensitive *avelut* is saturated with deep feelings of guilt. Quite a few of the injunctions governing the observance of *shivah* (prohibitions against washing, ointments, wearing shoes, and sexual intimacy) are reminiscent of Yom Kippur, a day when the Jew quests for forgiveness.

What are the sins for which the mourner seeks expiation? These are in two areas, vis-à-vis man (the departed) and vis-à-vis God.

Teshuvah vis-à-vis Man

Man is usually late in value judgments. His appreciation of persons, things, and events is a product of hindsight. In retrospection, man discovers the precise value of someone who was but is no longer with him. This delayed understanding and appreciation is painfully tragic. While the departed was near and we could communicate, we were only partially perceptive of his (her) identity. Our awareness of his specialness, as someone vital and precious to us, comes at the very instant he departs and withdraws into a mist of remoteness. Only then do we inquire with painful longing, "Who was he who brightened my days? What did he mean to me? Why do I feel so bereft and disoriented?''

These and similar questions, which descend in droves upon the grieving, expiating mourner, are extremely soul-searing, since they are saturated with guilt feelings. "Why didn't I ask these questions yesterday or yesteryear? Why wasn't I more expressive, more helpful, more appreciative?" Their image sparkles teasingly from afar. We extend our arms to embrace the departed, but a widening gap stretches between us. What exertions or treasures we would now readily expend for only five minutes with them, to open our hearts and minds to them, to make amends, to say what was left unsaid, to do what had been neglected. If only we could . . . but, alas, it is too late. Eulogists and mourners try to build bridges across the gap but, frustratingly, in vain. The disciples of Elijah went out to seek their master after his ascension in the tempest. Three days they sought him upon the mountains and in the valleys. They sought but could not find him (II Kings 2:17–18).[1]

In speaking of guilt, we are not referring to those who were neglectful or callous; such people will rarely look back with remorse. Our analysis is directed at those who were seemingly exemplary in their filial performance, yet are plagued with feelings of insufficiency in their hearts. They realize how fragmentary was their relationship. They bemoan opportunities lost forever. He who does not ache with such emotions is lacking in the experiential essence of *avelut*.

The Talmud in Ber. 42b[2] tells us a strange story: When Rav (founder of the Babylonian academy of Sura) died, his disciples walked after his bier in the funeral procession. On their return trip, they stopped to eat bread by the Danak River. Completing their meal, they discussed the halakhic question whether the requirement of *zimun* (invitation), so as to recite grace as a cohesive unit, applied in this case, since they had joined each other haphazardly. They were unable to resolve the problem. Whereupon Rav Ada bar Ahava rose and made another rent in his garment, which he had torn previously in grief, and said,

"Rav is dead and we haven't even learned from him the elementary rules of saying grace!" They discovered the greatness of their master and their dependence on him on the day they buried him. Sensing anew the depth of their loss, they were ready to give their lives for even the briefest opportunity to speak to him again.

How sad and ironic! They had studied under his tutelage for many long years and had been with him daily. He had trained their minds, fashioned their outlook, and had opened up to them vast vistas of thought. They had paid homage to him as the great master of the Diaspora, but even they did not discern Rav's stature and status. Now he had vanished from their midst and they tore their garments anew, reflecting an additional dimension of loss. Such ex post facto judgments are the saddest of life's experiences. How tragically elusive are even those who are close to us!

The *Rosh HaYeshivah* was preparing his annual *kinus teshuvah shiur,* which regularly drew thousands of listeners. He had been totally immersed in his material over the course of many hours, when he felt the hovering presence of his father and lifelong Rebbe, the Gaon Reb Moshe, *z. t. l.* "Oh my father," he said, "I have arrived at some fine insights about the laws of Yom Kippur and the *mitzvah* of *shofar.* Some of these ideas may please you, while others you will reject." He spoke to him beseechingly, even as the visitation was receding, leaving him with painful longing and emptiness. The days of yesteryear could not be recaptured. Oh, if only he could have several minutes of Talmudic discourse with him.!

Teshuvah vis-à-vis God

The mourner also feels guilty as regards his own religious identity. Our Sages had varied opinions about death. Was man originally intended upon creation to be mortal (Ex. R. 2:4),[3] or did he become mortal as a result of his demonstrated vulnerability to sin, by Adam and Eve and their descendants (Shab.

58b)⁴ (B. Bat. 75b)?⁵ Are not all men susceptible to sin, "for there is not a righteous man upon the earth who does [only] good and sins not" (Eccles. 7:20).⁶

The all-pervasive judgment is that death per se reflects the moral imperfection which is indigenous to all mankind, and that if man were perfect, if he did not inevitably fall short, he could elude death or assuage its sting. The prophet Isaiah projected a vision of the eschatological world when men will attain perfection and death will finally be defeated. "He will destroy death forever. And the Lord God will wipe the tears away from all faces" (Isa. 25:8).⁷ In the end of days, man will overcome his mortality.

In *avelut,* we ponder the relatedness of death to sin, and we reflect on the moral tenor of our life, noting its shortcomings and repenting of its failures. We think of our mortality and of our accountability and of the pressing need for religious reorientation. Kohelet counseled, "It is better [beneficial] to visit a house of mourning than a house of feasting; for that is the end of all men and the living will reflect thoughtfully" (Eccles. 7:2).⁸

The Sefer Hahinnukh explicitly equates *avelut* with *teshuvah.* "When he suffers the death of a near kin to whom he is emotionally bound, the Torah requires certain acts which concentrate his thoughts on his grief and he will realize that his grief relates to sinfulness. 'For the Eternal does not afflict or grieve the children of men' [Lam. 3:33]. When one reflects upon this, he will set his mind to *teshuvah* and will mend his ways as he could, but the wicked ascribe death to chance, saying 'that what befalls man and beast is alike; that the same fate is for both; as one dies so does the other' [Eccles. 3:19]."⁹ *Shivah, sheloshim,* and the *Kaddish* reject this nihilistic pessimism but affirm that the world is governed by a righteous God whose ways are often inscrutable (*Tzidduk Hadin*).

That mourning is equated with *teshuvah* is implicit in the practice in Talmudic days of *avelim* being required to overturn their couches (beds), *kefiyat hamitah.* Bar Kapara explained the symbolism: God said, "I have set My image upon them, but because of their sins, I have upset it. Let [therefore] your couches be overturned" (M. K. 15b).[10] Rashi explains that the image refers to God's spiritual image, *tzelem Elohim*, which is bestowed upon all mankind but is tarnished through sin.

Bar Kapara's explanation becomes intelligible if we note that in Talmudic and Midrashic semantics, the word *mitah* (bed, couch) represents one's progeny and, more specifically, man's role as a father and teacher, as a progenitor and as a pedagogue (i.e., *shemma yesh pasul b'mitati*, Pes. 5b).[11] He is the link between the past and the future on both the biological and spiritual levels, in the transmission of the tradition, *Mesorah*. The *mitah* is the "agent" in the procreative process and the seat from which learning is imparted. If a man (or woman) has failed to discharge this twofold duty, he has diminished the image, and punishment, possibly sorrow, may follow. The overturned *mitah* represents the *avel's* humble confession of unrealized potentiality or outright failure and a plea for forgiveness.

Overturning the *mitah* was later replaced by the custom (*Minhag*) of turning mirrors to the wall or covering them. The symbolism is the same as with the overturned *mitah*, namely, that our image is not as lustrous as it should be. The period of mourning suggests human failure, and covering the mirror is a form of *vidui*.[12]

"From Afar the Lord Appeared to Me"

The act of repentance partakes of the same nostalgic yearnings as experienced by the mourner for his departed. For the penitent also mourns the loss of a precious comradeship, the departure of Divine closeness. "From afar the Lord appeared to me; and with an everlasting love I have loved Him" (Jer. 31:2).[13] The penitent sees God far away, at an immeasurable distance. Once God was close, but he was blind and unappreciative. When he was devout, life was meaningful and comforting; there were intermittent moments of holiness. But then he became bored, distracted, and subverted, straying almost absentmindedly. He immersed himself in the here and now, with its immediate gratifications. He squandered God's comradeship; he relinquished what was most precious.

At first, the alienation was hardly perceived, its effects only vaguely discerned, as with mourners who only feel the finality of their loss after *shivah* and *sheloshim*. Gradually, it dawned upon him that he had lost the central pillar which provided stability and meaning to his life. "I feel banished. I have nobody to plead with, no one to cry to from the depths. The gates of heaven are closed to me. My path is twisted." But suddenly, the wonder takes place. "From afar the Lord appeared to me." From an infinite distance, he hears the soft whisper, "an everlasting love I have loved you." God, too, bemoans the separation. He, too, is lonely. He is waiting patiently. We are spiritual mourners when we sin, but the road to reconciliation is open to us, however distant and formidable.

The departed cannot come back, though we partially assuage the pain through the rites of *avelut*. But in *teshuvah* vis-à-vis God, the Torah assures us, "If you search there for the Lord your God, you will find Him, if only you seek Him with all your heart and soul" (Deut. 4:20).[14]

On the Next Day—Mimaḥarat

Many a time the Torah, while telling us about sin, adds, "And it came to pass on the morrow," *vayehi mimaḥarat* (Ex. 32:30),[15] or "They rose up in the morning," *Vayashkimu baboker* (Num. 14:40),[16] informing us that the next day they did repent. Yesterday they were insensitive and hard, shameful and rebellious, but today there is renewed openness and heightened receptivity. There is a *mimaḥarat,* a next day for rebuilding bridges of reconciliation. This is the great *ḥesed* of *teshuvah*.

הערות לפרק 13

1 **מלכים־ב ב, יז־יח**: וישלחו חמשים איש ויבקשו שלשה ימים ולא מצאהו... ויאמר אליהם, הלוא אמרתי אליכם אל תלכו.

2 **ברכות מב, ב**: כי נח נפשיה דרב, אזלו תלמידיו בתריה (רש"י — דקברוהו בעיר אחרת). כי הדדי, אמרי, ניזיל וניכול לחמא אנהר דנק. בתר דכרכי יתבי וקא מיבעיא להו, הסבו דוקא תנן אבל ישבו לא או דילמא כיון דאמרי ניזיל וניכול ריפתא בדוכתא פלניתא כי הסבו דמי (רש"י — דקתני, היו יושבים בלא הזמנת מקום הוא דלא הוי קביעות אבל אנו שהזמנינהו לכך, הוי קביעות ואחד מברך לכולן). לא הוי בידייהו. קם רב אדא בר אהבה, אהדר קריעה לאחוריה וקרע קריעה אחרינא. אמר: נח נפשיה דרב וברכת מזונא לא גמרינן (רש"י עכשיו כיום המיתה על שהיו צריכין להוראה ואין יודעין להורות).

3 **שמו"ר ב, ד**: ומשה היה — כל מי שכתוב בו "היה", מתוקן לכך. "הן אדם היה כאחד ממנו" (בראשית ג, כב), מתוקנת היתה המיתה לבא לעולם שנא' "וחושך על פני תהום" (שם א, ב), זו מיתה שמחשיך פני הבריות... מתחלת ברייתם נתקנו לכך.

4 **שבת נה, ב**: אמרו מלאכי השרת לפני הקב"ה: רבונו של עולם מפני מה קנסת מיתה על אדם הראשון? אמר להם: מצוה קלה צויתיו ועבר עליה. א"ל, והלא משה ואהרן שקיימו כל התורה כולה ומתו. א"ל מקרה אחד לצדיק ולרשע לטוב ולטהור (קהלת ט, ב). הוא דאמר כי האי תנא, דתניא. ר"ש בן אלעזר אומר, אף משה ואהרן בחטאם מתו שנאמר "יען לא האמנתם בי" (במדבר כ, יב), הא האמנתם בי, עדיין לא הגיע זמנכם ליפטר מן העולם.

5 **ב"ב עה, א**: אמר לו הקב"ה לחירם מלך צור, כך נסתכלתי (פי' רש"י — כשבראתי עולמי שאתה עתיד למרוד ולעשות אותך אלוה)... וקנסתי מיתה על אדם הראשון (משמע שאדם וחוה מתו מפני חטאי הדורות הבאים).

6 **קהלת ז, כ**: כי אדם אין צדיק בארץ אשר יעשה טוב ולא יחטא.

7 **ישעי' כה, ח**: בלע המות לנצח ומחה ה' אלקים דמעה מעל כל פנים.

8 **קהלת ז, ב**: טוב ללכת אל בית אבל מלכת אל בית משתה, כאשר הוא סוף כל האדם, והחי יתן אל לבו.

9 **ספר החנוך רסד**: על כן בבוא אליו עונש מקרה מות באחד מקרוביו אשר הטבע מחייב האהבה להם, תחייבנו התורה לעשות מעשים בעצמו אשר יעוררוהו לקבוע מחשבתו על הצער שהגיע אליו, ואז ידע ויתבונן בנפשו, כי עונותיו גרמו לו להגיע אליו הצער ההוא. כי השם לא יענה מלבו ויגע בני איש (איכה ג, לג), כי אם מצד חטאים... ובתת האדם אל לבו ענין זה במעשה האבלות, ישית דעתו לעשות תשובה

ויכשיר מעשיו כפי כוחו. והמתחכמים הכופרים... יתלו מות בני איש למקרה הזמן, כי מקרה האדם והבהמה אחד להם, כמות זה, כן מות זה (קהלת ג, יט).

10 **מועד קטן טו, א**: אבל חייב בכפיית המטה. דתני בר קפרא: דמות דיוקנו נתתי בהן ובעוונותיהם הפכתיה, כפו מטותיהם עליה (פי׳ רש״י — "דמות דיוקנו" בצלם אלקים עשה את האדם).

11 **פסחים נו, א**: ביקש יעקב לגלות קץ הימין ונסתלקה ממנו שכינה, אמר: "שמא חס ושלום יש במטתי (בבני) פסול, כאברהם שיצא ממנו ישמעאל ואבי יצחק שיצא ממנו עשו, אמרו לו בניו: שמע ישראל (לאביהם היו אומרים) ה׳ אלקינו ה׳ אחד", אמרו: כשם שאין בלבך אלא אחד, כך אין בלבנו אלא אחד" (ראה ויק״ר לו, ד "אבל יעקב מטתו שלימה, כל בניו צדיקים).

12 **שו״ע יו״ד סי׳ שפ״ז ס״ב**: עכשיו לא נהגו בכפיית המטה; כתוב בשו״ת "דודאי השדה" (סי׳ עח) בשם חתם סופר, דעכשיו נוהגין לכסות המראה, דזהו במקום כפיית המטה. ובירושלמי (מו״ק פ״ג) מפורש, הפכו הסרסר (agent), דהיינו המטה שהוא הסרסר בין איש לאשתו לצורך יצירת הולד. והמראות הצובאות ג״כ סרסורים הם ולכן מכסין אותן (גם נראה בהם דמות דיוקנן, ע״כ מהפכין — גנזי יוסף קמח).

13 **ירמי׳ לא, ב**: מרחוק ה׳ נראה לי, ואהבת עולם אהבתיך.

14 **דברים ד, כט**: ובקשתם משם את ה׳ אלקיך ומצאת כי תדרשנו בכל לבבך ובכל נפשך.

15 **במדבר יד, מ**: וישכימו בבקר, ויעלו אל ראש ההר לאמר, הננו, ועלינו אל המקום אשר אמר ה׳, כי חטאנו.

16 **שמות לב, ל. לג, ד**: ויהי ממחרת ויאמר משה אל העם, אתם חטאתם חטאה גדולה... וישמע העם את הדבר הרע הזה ויתאבלו (עשו תשובה).

Chapter XIV

RABBI AKIBA'S HOMILY ON TESHUVAH

Rabbi Akiba said: "You are fortunate, Israel! Before whom do you cleanse yourself, and who cleanses you [from your transgressions]? Your Heavenly Father; as it is said, 'And I shall sprinkle (*v'zarakti*) clean water upon you, and you shall be clean' (Ezek. 36:25); and it says again, 'The hope of Israel (*mikveh Yisrael*)' (Jer. 17:13)—just as the ritual bath (*mikveh*) cleanses the unclean, so too does the Holy One, blessed be He, cleanse Israel" (Yoma 8:9).[1] (Rabbi Akiba here translated the words *mikveh Yisrael* in the sense that God is the purifer of Israel, like *tevillah* (immersion) in a reservoir of water. The more usual understanding of *mikveh Yisrael* is that He is *tikvat Yisrael*, Israel's final hope.)

Rabbi Akiba is formulating a significant equation; the state of sinfulness (*het, avon, pesha*) is equated with *tumah*, ritual uncleanness; also, the act of *teshuvah* equals *taharah*, ritual purification. It is like a mathematical equation, sin = *tumah* and *teshuvah* = *taharah*. We know that for most types of *tumah* (*zav, zavah, sheretz, metzora, yoledet*), the *taharah* consists of immersion in a *mikveh* (*tevillah*). For the more severe *tumah* of *tumat-met* (Num. 19), the *taharah* additionally requires *haza'ah* with the waters of the *Parah Adumah*. There are, thus, two types of purification, *mikveh* and *haza'ah* (*v'zarakti*), and R. Akiba's homily mentions both. Correspondingly, there are also two types of *teshuvah*, one comparable to the *mikveh* purification and the other to *haza'ah*.

Two Types of Taharah—Two Types of Teshuvah

The two types of *taharah* differ from each other significantly. *Mikveh* (*tevillah*) requires the personal initiative of the unclean person; only he can do it; if he is lazy or fearful of water, his status cannot be changed; the defiled must perform the act himself. He descends into the water, bows his head, bends his knees, and submerges in a sea, river, or any kosher *mikveh*. He then rises a *tahor* (*yarad, v'taval, v'alah*). This is symbolic of what transpires in *teshuvah*. The *baal teshuvah* must descend from his haughty arrogance and pride, bow his head in remorse, submerge himself in repentance, and then rise with his sins atoned. If the penitent approaches his *teshuvah* with his head aloft, only reluctantly regretful and with ego uncowed, his repentance is ineffective, just as being physically inflexible in a *mikveh* renders the *taharah* invalid.

The opposite is the case with the *haza'ah* where the *tamei* cannot sprinkle upon himself; it must always be "and the clean person shall sprinkle upon the unclean" (Num. 19:19), *v'hizah hatahor al hatamei*. He cannot cleanse himself; only a *tahor* can do it for him. If he sprinkles upon himself, the purification is inoperative. *Mikveh* is self-liberation; *haza'ah* must involve another.

R. Akiba is teaching that there are two types of *teshuvah*, one that is comparable to *mikveh*, which can be attained through one's own initiative, and the other, which is like *haza'ah*, where God's helping hand is needed. The Talmud records the story of Eliezer ben Durdyah, who, recognizing that he was deeply steeped in sin, sought intercessors to help him do *teshuvah*. "Seek mercy for me," *baksho alei rahamim*, he pleaded, until he realized that "it all depends upon my own initiative" (A.Z. 17a).[2] Neither the mountains, the sun and moon, nor the stars and planets could intercede for him. He had to muster his own resolve to achieve repentance, which he finally attained. In the *mikveh-teshuvah*, God waits for the wicked and is eager that he return to righteousness, *Hatzofeh l'rasha v'hafetz b'hitzdeko* (*V'chol Ma'aminim piyut*), but God doesn't help him. He merely opens the door to *teshuvah, hapote'ah sha'ar l'dofkei vitshuvah*.³ He waits for him; "Thou dost wait for him until his dying day; if he repents, thou dost readily accept him"—V'ad yom moto tihakheh lo, im Yashuv, mi-yad tikablo.⁴ But it is up to man; if he is too proud, nothing will result. God will wait, *Tichakey Lo,* but that is all; if he repents, he will be accepted. *Im Yashov, mi-yad tikablo,* but God sends no reception committee, no *kabbalat panim,* to beseech his entrance. This is the *mikveh-Teshuvah.*

Haza'ah-Teshuvah differs sharply. Here God helps him, tugs at him, and suggests to him the beauty of *teshuvah* and the absurdity of sin. "Thou dost reach out Thy hand to the transgressors; Thy right hand is extended to receive repentant sinners" (*Ne'ilah*).⁵ Here God is not a *tzofeh l'rasha* but rather a *noten yad;* He raises him. God is his teacher, his leader and purifier, promising him great rewards.

It is as if a man were running and there is a wide ditch before him. He must jump over it, and God extends His hand, to lift him over, a *noten yad,* and carries him to the other side, to *teshuvah.* God helps him because the sinner is confounded by the seemingly impassable gulf between him and *teshuvah* and despairs of attaining it. God here is a *mishtatef,* a participant, to help him enter the *Shaarei Teshuvah* (gates of repentance).

That *haza'ah* suggests a Divine involvement is taught by the Tanchuma: on the verse, *v'asaf ish tahor* (Num. 19:19), the Tanchuma adds, "This is the Holy One."⁶ The *v'hizah hatahor al ha-tamei* refers to the Almighty, who is the ultimate *metaher* in *tumat-met* and is, according to the analogy of Rabbi Akiba, also an active participant in the *haza'ah* type of teshuvah.

Difference Between Teshuvah All Year and Teshuvah on Yom Kippur

Teshuvah is efficacious all year, and the primary purpose of rabbinically enacted fast days, and of fast days which are privately assumed, is to induce self-searching repentance. Maimonides states this clearly, *V'davar zeh midarkhei teshuvah,* referring to fast days (Hil. Ta'anit 1:2). But all *teshuvah* except on Yom Kippur is of the *mikveh* type, where man must raise himself while God is a *tzofeh l'rasha*—He waits patiently without involvement. The Rambam calls the cleansing water of *mikveh, mei-haa'at* (Hil. Mikva'ot 11:12), waters of understanding, of self-recognition, and self-analysis, involving such known aspects of *teshuvah* as *hakoret hahet, haratah, bushah, kabbalah al ha-osid,* etc. These are parts of the *mei-hada'at* when the sinner is stricken in conscience and asks himself, "What have I done? I've ruined my life. I've lost my family, my prestige, my personal sense of value" This is the *mikveh* cleansing all year. All year it's *mikveh Yisrael.*

On Yom Kippur, however, the *taharah* is easier. It is a *haza'ah* kind of *teshuvah.* God helps him. Man is led back to himself—his real self. The *Kedushat Ha-Yom* provides a *v'zorakti aleikhem mayim tehorim.* God intercedes to bring him to a state of *lifnei Hashem titharu* (Lev. 16:30). The *Ne'ilah* climax capsulates this clearly in the words, *Atah noten yad l'poshim.*

The Two Haftarot

In Isaiah, there are two portions on *teshuvah* which are used as Haftorot for fast days. For a *ta'anit tzibbur* of the entire year, *Dirshu Hashem b'himatzo* (chap. 55:6–56:7) is read: "Seek ye the Lord while He may be found. Call upon Him while He is near; let the wicked forsake his way and the man of iniquity his thoughts. And let him return unto the Lord, and He will have compassion upon him, and to our God, for He will abundantly pardon."[7] Here it is the penitent who is searching for God; he must take the initiative. God once called the first man, *ayekah,* "Where art thou?" (Gen. 3:9), but he hid and didn't answer. Since then, God calls man only on Yom Kippur. If man wants God, let him find the road himself, and the road is often zigzagged and not a highway for easy travel. This prophetic portion emphasizes personal initiative, *v'yashuv el Hashem,* it is the *mikveh-teshuvah,* which characterizes teshuvah all year.

Tumah precludes one from entering the sanctuary; *taharah* reopens the road. "Jerusalem," the psalmist tells us, "is surrounded by mountains" (Ps. 125:2). *Yerushalayim harim saviv lah.* One must climb hills in order to get to the *Mikdash;* he may fall but he rises again, perserveringly, as one would seek to ascend Mount Everest. Eventually, he will reach the peak. Similarly, with the penitent, it is a case of *dirshu Hashem b'himatzo*—persistent effort; personal initiative; he hears no *Ayekah* from Hashem—no words of urging. This is the *mikveh teshuvah* where God is only a *pote'ah sha'ar l'dofkei vitshuvah;* the door is open, but man must find the portal himself and manage to get through. This is the first Haftarah.

The Yom Kippur Haftarah strikes a different theme. *Solu, solu, panu darekh.* "The Lord says: Make a path, clear the way, remove every obstacle from my people's path" (Isa. 57:14).[8] Here God says to Himself that He is breaking a road, clearing the encumbering jungle, opening a broad highway for the pentitent to travel with ease to attain his *teshuvah.* Indeed, God welcomes and encourages him: *Shalom, shalom larahok v'lakarov,* "peace for those who have strayed far and near," *amar Hashem u'refativ* (v. 19), "and they shall be healed." God is *mekabel panim* (welcomes) every penitent; this is *haza'ah teshuvah;* God is a *noten yad;* this is the great distinctive privilege of *itzumu shel yom* of Yom Kippur.

Two Types of Sin

We have established that there are two types of *teshuvah* corresponding to the two types of *taharah.* This is because there are two types of sin, one requiring *mikveh-teshuvah* and the other, *haza'ah-teshuvah.*

There are sins, ethical or ritual, which can be ascribed to external circumstances, the sinner succumbing to outer temptations. The sin does not emerge from his personality, *penimiyut;* his natural bent and philosophy are wholesome, but he yields easily to diverse pressures—economic considerations (*parnaseh*), social trends ideological fads and fashions of the day, charismatic friends, etc. Sin is not rooted in any perversion in his personality or ideology. Indeed, he does not proudly identify with his sin and is somewhat apologetic. He stumbled into it.

One can compare sin to a person falling and injuring himself. The doctor seeks to ascertain whether someone pushed him, causing him to trip over an obstacle in the road, or whether perhaps, his fall was due to an internal dizziness, a vertigo, a loss of equilibrium. What difference does it make how he fell? The answer is that if the cause was external, his bruise or broken limb can be corrected with relative ease. The case is not serious. But if it was due to some internal disorder, then the situation is of much greater concern. The malady must be diagnosed and treated before good health is restored.

Externally caused sin can be undone by a *mikveh* type of *teshuvah* where the penitent asserts his will and character and resolutely reaches out to God. Man can do it himself, and God waits patiently for him to take the initiative.

The *tefillah zakkah,* recited by many prior to *Kol Nidrei,* describes such a sinner accurately: "And now, my God, it is clear to You that I had not intended with all my sins to rebel against you. Rather I followed the counsel of my evil inclinations, which ensnared me, and I, being weak in will, could not withstand the temptations, the travails of earning a livelihood, of feeding my household, the tensions and demands of the times, and all these corrupted me."[9] This prayer is a plea of self-defense. Such externally induced sins can be undone through personal initiative. If one has character, he will declare these sins alien to himself and will resolutely reject them.

The second type of sin emerges out of one's false Weltanschauung, a false *hashkafat olam*, a system of values which is deeply imbedded in him which he cannot easily undo because his inner core is corrupted. What he needs is an uprooting of personality and a transformation of his central value system.

For this, one needs God. It is not the amount of sin but the type of sin which decides whether its eradication can be achieved by personal effort or if God's help is also needed. The therapy, whether *mikveh-teshuvah* or *haza'ah-teshuvah,* is determined by the nature of the spiritual ailment. For external bruises, the *mikveh-teshuvah* suffices; an internal infection, where it is psychologically deep in the structure of one's personality, requires a *haza'ah-teshuvah* treatment.

Rabbi Akiba's Homily Explained

This, therefore, is what Rabbi Akiba said: "Before whom do you cleanse yourself, and who cleanses you?" Why two references here to *taharah?* Wouldn't it have been more meaningful for Rabbi Akiba to refer first to *taharah* and then to *kaparah,* as follows: "Who cleanses you, and who forgives you?"[10] Why two clauses dealing with *taharah?* The answer is now clear; he is referring to two types of *taharah. Lifnei mi atah metarin,* "before whom are you purifying yourself?" refers to *Mikveh Yisrael* type of *teshuvah,* where the penitent can take off his *bigdei Hatzoim,* his dirty garments, himself. That is the way of *teshuvah* all year, especially on a *ta'anit tzibur.* Man is the *metaher,* but God is the *mehaper.* But on Yom Kippur, God says, "Let's both of us be involved in *taharah.* You do a little and I'll do a little." God works with man. And only then is *kaparah* achieved. All year God waits, *Techakeh Lo,* but on Yom Kippur, in addition to *Lifnei mi Atem Metaharim,* we add *Umi Metaher Etchem.* For this, the appropriate verse is *vezarakti aleikhem mayim tehorim,* a *haza'ah* type of *teshuvah,* in addition to *Mikveh Yisrael.*

הערות לפרק 14

1 **יומא פ"ח, מ"ט:** אמר רבי עקיבא, אשריכם ישראל, לפני מי אתם מטהרין ומי מטהר אתכם אביכם שבשמים, שנאמר "וזרקתי עליכם מים טהורים וטהרתם" (יחזקאל לו, כה) ואומר, "מקוה ישראל ה'" (ירמי׳ יז, יג) — מה מקוה מטהר את הטמאים אף הקב"ה מטהר את ישראל (ר׳ עקיבא דורש "מקוה" במובן מקוה מים).

2 **ע"ז יז, א:** אמרו עליו ר׳ אלעזר בן דורדיא . . . אמר: הרים וגבעות בקשו עלי רחמים . . . שמים וארץ בקשו עלי רחמים, חמה ולבנה בקשו עלי רחמים . . . כוכבים ומזלות, בקשו עלי רחמים . . . אמר: אין הדבר תלוי אלא בי, הניח ראשו על ברכיו וגעה בבכיה עד שיצאתה נשמתו, יצאה בת קול ואמרה: ר׳ אלעזר בן דורדיא מזומן לחיי עולם הבא.

3 **פיוט וכל מאמנים:** הפותח שער לדופקי בתשובה, וכל מאמינים שהוא פתוחה ידו, הצופה לרשע וחפץ בהצדקו.

4 **בונתנה תוקף:** ועד יום מותו תחכה לו, אם ישוב מיד תקבלו.

5 אתה נותן יד לפושעים, וימינך פשוטה לקבל שבים ותלמדנו להתודות וכו׳ (נעילה).

6 **תנחומא (בובר חקת ס, ב):** ואסף — זה הקב"ה, דכתיב "ונשא נס לגויים, ואסף נדחי ישראל (ישעי׳ י, יא): "איש" — זה הקב"ה, דכתיב "ה' איש מלחמה" (שמות טו).

7 **ישעי׳ נה, ו:** דרשו ה' בהמצאאו קראהו בהיותו קרוב, יעזוב רשע דרכו ואיש און מחשבותיו, וישוב אל ה' וירחמהו, ואל אלקינו כי ירבה לסלוח.

8 **ישעי׳ נז, יד-יט:** סולו סולו, פנו דרך הרימו מכשול מדרך עמי . . . שלום שלום לרחוק ולקרוב אמר ה' ורפאתיו.

9 **חיי אדם קמד, כ):** תפלת זכה: ועתה ד׳ אלקי, גלוי וידוע לפניך שלא נתכוונתי בכל החטאים והעונות להכעיס אותך ולמרוד כנגדך, אך הלכתי בעצת יצרי הרע אשר תמיד פורש רשת לרגלי ללכדני, ואני עני ואביון, תולעת ולא איש, כשל כחי לעמוד כנגדו, ועמל הפרנסה לפרנס את בני ביתי וטרדת הזמן ומקריו הם היו בעוכרי.

CHAPTER XV

THE HAFTARAH OF JONAH ON YOM KIPPUR

Why did our Sages select the Book of Jonah as the Haftarah, the prophetic portion, for the Yom Kippur *minḥah* service? An obvious answer is that Jonah demonstrates dramatically the inexhaustibility of God's forgiveness to repentant sinners. This *ḥesed* is extended even if the punitive sentence (*gezar din*) has already been decreed, as was the case with the people of Nineveh. The attribute of strict justice (*midat hadin*) is ever ready to defer to the attribute of mercy (*midat haraḥamim*). This theme is reassuringly appropriate for the closing hours of the holy day.

The association of Jonah with Yom Kippur may have a more historical and profound derivation. This prophetic text ascribes Nineveh's successful repentance not to their prayerful fasts, but to their moral regeneration. No placatory rituals or incantations opened for them "the gates of compassion," but their turning away from evil and their performance of righteous deeds.

In Mishnah Ta'anit 2:1, our Sages refer to the successful penitence of Nineveh in exhorting a similar return to justice and righteousness on the part of Israel as a means of effecting an end to an unrelieved drought in the Holy Land. On the last of a series of public fasts, the following procedure was followed: "They would bring out the ark to the town square and wood-ashes were strewn on the ark and on the head of the *nasi* [leader of the community] and on the head of the *av bet din* [leader of the court]. Everyone present [also] placed ashes on his head. The eldest among them addressed them with words of admonition, *divrei kivushim.* "Brethren! Of the people of Nineveh, it is not said, 'and God saw their sackcloth and fasting' but, 'and God saw their deeds, that they had turned from their evil ways' " (Jonah 3:6). [As] it says in the prophetic book, "rend your hearts, not your clothing, and turn unto the Lord" (Joel 2:13).[1]

The theme that penitence must concomitantly find its expression in moral living is most certainly needful on Yom Kippur, lest we be obsessed with the expiatory sufficiency of fasting and devotional ritual. The same message is also highlighted in the earlier Haftarah after *Shaharit,* where the prophet Isaiah decries, "Those who fast in strife and contention . . . is such the fast I desire? Is it bowing the head like a bulrush and lying in sackcloth and ashes? . . . This is the fast I desire, to unlock the fetters of wickedness and untie the cords of the oppressed, to share your bread with the hungry and take the wretched poor into your home" (58:5–7).[2]

The Universal Extension

There may be an additional reason for Jonah's association with Yom Kippur. It does more than illustrate the potency of genuine *teshuvah* and the moral improvement which is a requisite for repentance. Nineveh was the capital city of pagan Assyria, today known as Iraq. It was the country which would later, under Sennacherib in 722 B.C.E., besiege Jerusalem and exile the ten tribes. Yet God's compassion embraces all of humanity. He is a *mekabel teshuvah* not only from his covenantal people, but from all nations. The gates of atonement are widely open to all.

At the end of the book, God says to Jonah: "You took pity on the gourd [a tree with large leaves which God had prepared for Jonah to relieve him from the sun's discomfort; it later withered], for which you did not labor, nor did you make it grow, which came up in a night and perished overnight. And should I not have pity on Nineveh, that great city in which there are more than a hundred and twenty thousand persons who do not know their right hand from their left [children], and also many beasts" (4:10).³ The Yalkut records Jonah's response: "At that moment, Jonah fell upon his face and said, 'May the world continue to be governed by the attribute of mercy, as it says, 'To the Lord our God belongs compassion and forgiveness' (Dan. 9:9)."⁴

During the Yom Kippur services, our prayerful concerns are almost exclusively with our own people. We acknowledge God as "He who sanctified Israel and the Day of Atonement," *mekadesh yisrael v'yom hakippurim;* "Thou art the forgiver of Israel," *ki Atah salḥan l'yisrael;* "Oh, pardon the iniquity of this people, *Selaḥ na la'avon ha'am hazeh;* "We are Thy people and Thou art our God," *Ki anu amekha v'atah Elohenu.* We are often accused of being parochially clannish. This may be true, for otherwise we would have succumbed long ago, considering our historical vulnerability. But this self-involvement is not hermetically exclusionary. The universal emphasis is prominent in all our prayers, in Scripture, the Talmud, and the Midrash; and when opportunities were benign and conditions propitious, we have contributed far more than our proportionate share to the welfare of humanity.

Our Rosh Hashanah liturgy informs us that all mankind stands in judgment during this period of the year; *v'khal ba'ei olam ta'avir l'fanekha kivnei maron . . . v'tifkod nefesh kal chai* (*U-netanneh Tokef*). Indeed, the destiny of entire nations is determined: "On this day is decreed which countries are destined for the sword and which for peace, which for famine and which for plenty. On this day, every creature stands in judgment and is recorded for life or death." *V'al hamedinot bo ye'amar, ayzeh l'herev, v'ayzeh l'shalom, ayzeh l'ra'av v'ayzaeh l'sava. Uvriyot bo yifokaydo, l'hazkirom l'ḥayyim u'lamavet.*

It is, therefore, characteristic of the universal embrace of our faith that as the shadows of dusk descend on Yom Kippur day, after almost twenty-four hours of prayer for Israel, the Jew is alerted through the Book of Jonah, prior to the closing of "the heavenly gates" (*Ne'ilah*), that all humanity are God's children. We need to restate the universal dimension of our faith, especially when we are sorely persecuted and are apt to regard the world in purely confrontational terms.

Relating the Haftarah to the Keriah

The practice of adding a Haftarah from the prophets after the Pentateuchal *Sidrah* was, according to some scholars, established in the days of the Maccabees (200–150 B.C.E.), when the Syrian-Greek ruler over the Holy Land had prohibited the public reading from the Five Books of Moses, which is the basic source of Jewish Law. Our Sages, therefore, ordained that a selection from the prophets which is in some way suggestive or thematically related to the proscribed Torah reading be substituted.[5] The Haftarah selection is composed of at least twenty-one verses, corresponding to the minimal twenty-one verses required for the seven *aliyot,* of three verses each. The seven blessings surrounding the Haftarah are also reminiscent of the *shivah keru'im* (the minimal seven *aliyot*). Thereby, the Torah was not forgotten and a remembrance of the scheduled Torah reading was preserved for such time as the decree would be abrogated. When the Maccabees triumphed, the Pentateuchal reading was reinstated, but the Haftarah was retained.

The thematic kinship of *Maftir Yonah* and the Yom Kippur *Minḥah* reading, known as *Parashat Arayut* (unlawful marriages), needs to be explored. The relationship becomes apparent as we establish the appropriateness of this Torah reading for Yom Kippur afternoon.

The Torah reading is a forceful declaration of Jewish separatism even as the Book of Jonah is a counterbalance of Jewish universalism. Lest we misconstrue our separateness and distinctiveness as a license for callous indifference to other peoples, the Haftarah enlarges our scope of compassion and understanding.

The Torah reading begins as follows: "And the Lord spoke to

Moses, saying: Speak to the children of Israel and say unto them: I am the Lord. You shall not imitate the practices of the land of Egypt where you dwelt, or of the land of Canaan to which I am taking you; nor shall you follow their ways; My rules alone shall you observe and faithfully follow My laws; I the Lord am your God. . . . You shall not approach anyone who is of your own kin, to uncover nakedness, I am the Lord" (Lev. 18:1–6).[6] The chapter exhorts Israel to shun the licentious ways of the heathens of Egypt and Canaan. This prescribes an ideological and behavioral separation and is an injunction against acculturation and assimilation. Distinctiveness is to be the mark of our identity.

The allure of Egypt, the most cultured and technologically developed society of that day, was to be resisted, as were the pastoral pagan charms of seductive Canaan with its nature worship. These are ever-recurring types of cultural temptation. There are those who are mesmerized by the technological marvels of highly developed civilizations with their culture and art; others reject such impersonal and mechanistic societies with their heartless exploitation and imperialism. They seek, instead, the kinship of a relaxed, less rapacious society of libertinism and closeness to nature. The Torah, therefore, insists that both be rejected as alien to the Jewish spirit. Artifacts of man's creativity are not to be worshipped, and regression to childlike simplicity or animallike sensuality violates the spiritual dimension in man. The chapter particularly denounces the sexual immorality and perversion which were widely rampant among heathen people and declares such decadence reprehensible for Israel.

Separation has been the Jewish way since time immemorial. To be different inevitably means to be apart. In Moses' day, the Israelites were described as "a people that dwells alone" (Num. 23:9). In our day, the reconstitution of the State of Israel was intended to create a separate entity with its singular ideology and way of life. Israel is an affirmation of separatism and reflects the refusal of the Jewish people to be submerged into anonymity among the nations. Thus does Israel find itself today alone, an historical role indigenous to its very identity.

The *Parashat Arayot* was, according to Rashi, read on Yom Kippur "due to the lapses from these laws and the urge that tends to overpower" (Meg. 31a).[7] Tosafot adds, "on Yom Kippur it was customary for women to adorn themselves in honor of the holiday" (ibid.).[8] Both Rashi and Tosafot seem to be alluding to a custom of Talmudic days on Yom Kippur and on the Fifteenth of Av, for "maidens of Jerusalem to go out dressed in white, borrowed clothing, in order not to embarrass one who had none, and dance in the vineyards. And what did they say? 'Young men, lift up your eyes and behold what you choose for yourself' " (Mishnah Ta'anit 4:8).[9] Thereby did young men and women meet and choose mates. The Torah text about chastity, morality, and forbidden marriages is, therefore, most timely for Yom Kippur afternoon.

During all of Yom Kippur the emphasis is on Israel's particularism. God's compassionate beneficence to Israel is beseeched. But as Yom Kippur draws to a close, we remind ourselves that there is a wider world sorely in need of atonement, a world with more serious sins than Jews have ever perpetrated, since its peoples have had more power to inflict their rapaciousness, unrestrained by the humanistic refinements instilled by the Torah. Our Sages, therefore, prescribed the reading about Nineveh's repentance as a balance to the Torah reading which preached an insular outlook. We read of forgiveness, not of Judah or Ephraim but of Nineveh, the capital of Assyria. Even as Jewish singularity is affirmed, we decry chauvinism; self-interest need not breed disdain for others. We are members of the larger family of man.

Similar Balance in the Haggadah

The Passover *Seder* is an exclusively Jewish commemoration. "This is the ordinance of the Passover: no alien shall eat thereof; no uncircumcised person shall partake thereof" (Ex.

12:43, 49).[10] In the Haggadah, we relive our humble beginnings and our sufferings in Egypt. We take note that our history is replete with many other persecutions and tyrants who similarly sought our destruction. "For not one tyrant only has risen up against us to destroy us, but in every generation tyrants have sought to destroy us, and the Holy One, blessed be He, has delivered us from their hand."[11] We implore, "Pour out Thy wrath upon the nations that know Thee not, for they have devoured Jacob and laid waste his habitation" (*Shefokh Ḥamatkha*). The *Seder* speaks of an apartness in Egypt, and our Sages interpret the verse "And he became there a great nation" (*l'goy gadol*) as meaning, "This teaches that the Israelites were distinguishable there" (*metzuyanim*—as a nation apart).[12]

Such insular emphasis can motivate an unremitting anger and animosity against the world's other peoples, for they have persistently been our persecutors and we have been their victims. All evening the Haggadah proceeds without respite in acknowledging our painful experiences in history, but with unflagging faith in our eventual redemption.

But suddenly, before we conclude, we recite an ancient and beautiful adoration: *Nishmat Kal Ḥai*—"The breath of every living being shall bless Thy name, O Lord our God."[13] We ecstatically envision all of the countries of the world joining in a grand symphony of homage to God. We move from Jewish redemption to the ultimate salvation of all mankind, and we pray for the day when "every mouth shall give thanks and every tongue shall swear allegiance unto You. . . . Every knee shall bow to You." Suddenly the horizon of the Jew is broadened, and he sees himself involved with the welfare of all mankind when, hopefully, "the Lord shall be King over all the earth; on that day the Lord shall be One and His name One" (Zech. 14:9).[14]

הערות לפרק 15

1. **תענית ב, א**: סדר תעניות כיצד? מוציאין את התיבה לרחובה של עיר, ונותנין אפר מקלה על גבי התבה, ובראש הנשיא, ובראש אב ב"ד, וכל אחד ואחד נותן בראשו, הזקן שבהן אומר לפניהם דברי כבושין: "אחינו!! לא נאמר באנשי נינוה "וירא אלקים את שקם ואת תעניתם", אלא "וירא האלקים את מעשיהם כי שבו מדרכם הרעה" (ג, ו), ובקבלה הוא אומר, "קרעו לבבכם ואל בגדיכם" (יואל ב, יג).

2. **ישעי' נח, ה-ז**: הכזה יהיה צום אבחרהו: יום ענות אדם נפשו? הלכף כאגמן ראשו! ושק ואפר יציע? הלזה תקרא צום ויום רצון לה'? הלא זה צום אבחרהו. פתח חרצבות רשע, התר אגדות מוטה, ושלח רצוצים חפשים, וכל מוטה תנתקו. הלא פרס לרעב לחמך, ועניים מרודים תביא בית. כי תראה ערום וכסיתו ומבשרך לא תתעלם.

3. **יונה ד, י**: ויאמר ה', אתה חסת על הקיקיון אשר לא עמלת בו ולא גדלתו, שבן לילה היה ובן לילה אבד. ואני לא אחוס על נינוה, העיר הגדולה אשר יש בו הרבה משתים עשרה רבו אדם אשר לא ידע בין ימינו לשמאלו ובהמה רבה.

4. **יל"ש**: באותה שעה נפל על פניו ואמר, הנהג עולמך במדת הרחמים דכתי' "לה' אלקינו הרחמים והסליחות" (דניאל ט, ט).

5. **אבודרהם, לבוש, תוי"ט מגילה ג, ד**: טעמא דהפטרות כתוב בספר תשבי שרש פטר. שמצא כתוב שאנטיוכס הרשע מלך יון גזר על ישראל שלא יקראו בתורה ברבים. מה עשו ישראל? לקחו פרשה א' מנביאים שעניינה דומה לעניין מ"ש בפרשה של שבת ההיא. ועתה, אף שבטלה הגזירה, המנהג הזה אינו בטל (ולקריאת הנביאים שלא חשבו הגוים מעיקר הדת, לא חששו).

6. **ויקרא יח, א**: וידבר ה' אל משה לאמר: דבר אל בני ישראל ואמרת אליהם, אני ה' אלקיכם, כמעשה ארץ מצרים אשר ישבתם בה לא תעשו וכמעשה ארץ כנען אשר אני מביא אתכם שמה לא תעשו, ובחוקותיהם לא תלכו. את "משפטי תעשו ואת חוקותי תשמרו ללכת בהם, אני ה' אלקיכם — איש איש אל כל שאר בשרו לא תקרבו לגלות ערוה, אני ה'".

7. **רש"י, מגילה לא, א**: קוראין בעריות — שמי שיש עבירות בידו, יפרוש מהן. לפי שהעריות עבירה מצויה, שנפשו של אדם מחמדתן ויצרו תקופו.

8. **תוס' שם**: לפי שהנשים מקושטות בשביל כבוד היום לפיכך צריך להזכירם שלא יכשלו בהן.

9. **תענית פ"ד מ"ח**: אמר רבן שמעון בן גמליאל: לא היו ימים טובים לישראל כחמשה עשר באב וכיום הכפורים שבהן בנות ירושלים

יוצאות בכלי לבן שאולין שלא לבייש את מי שאין לו, כל הכלים טעונים טבילה, ובנות ירושלים יוצאות וחולות בכרמים ומה היו אומרות? בחור! שא נא עיניך וראה מה אתה בורר לך.

10 **שמות יב, מג-מח**: זאת חקת הפסח, כל בן נכר לא יאכל בו . . . וכל ערל לא יאכל בו.

11 **הגדה**: והיא שעמדה לאבותינו ולנו, שלא אחד בלבד עמד עלינו לכלותינו, אלא שבכל דור ודור עומדים עלינו לכלותינו והקב"ה מצילנו מידם.

12 **דברים כו, ה**: ויהי שם לגוי גדול — מלמד שהיו ישראל מצויינים שם, שלא שנו את שמם, ולא שנו את דתם ולשונם בכל השנים הרבות אשר ישבו שם. והיו תמיד גוי מפני עצמם (ספרי).

13 **סידור**: נשמת כל חי תברך שמך ה' אלקינו . . . כי כל פה לך יודה וכל לשון לך תשבע וכל ברך לך תכרע.

14 **זכרי' יד, ט**: והיה ה' למלך על כל הארץ, ביום ההוא יהיה ה' אחד ושמו אחד.

Chapter XVI

HAKAFOT—MOVING IN CIRCLES

The verse "I wash my hands in innocence, so that I may encircle Your altar, Hashem" (Ps. 26:10)[1] is an admonition that before we approach the altar in worship, we should cleanse ourselves of evil deeds.[2] You cannot come to God with dirty hands. Though this teaching is widely applied, Rashi and the Yalkut relate the verse specifically to the festival of Sukkot because only on this holiday do we circle the altar, *Hakafot*. The verse, according to Rashi, informs us that "the [*mitzvah* of the] *Arba Minim* may not be acquired through theft. A stolen *lulav* is invalid."[3]

The Yalkut elaborates further: "*I wash my hands in innocence*—the *lulav* was acquired through purchase, not through theft, as it says: *U'lekaḥtem lakhem,* 'You shall acquire for yourself [legitimately] on the first day of Sukkot, [Lev. 23:30]; *so that I may encircle your altar, Hashem*—Every day [of Sukkot], they encircled the *mizbe'aḥ* [altar] once. What was the manner of the *Hakafah?* All Jews, old and young, held the *lulav* in their right hand and the *etrog* in their left hand, and they did one *Hakafah*. That day [Hoshana Rabba] they did seven *Hakafot*. R. Ḥiyah said: The number seven is reminiscent of Jericho [which was encircled seven times, initiating the conquest of *Eretz Yisrael,* whose produce the *Arba Minim* celebrate— Joshua 6:4]. This was the procedure when there was a *mizbe'aḥ*. Nowadays, [the Temple having been destroyed), the *ḥazan* stands, like an angel of God, with a *Sefer Torah* in his arms, and the congregation encircles him as it had [previously] the *mizbe'aḥ*" (Yalkut, Ps. 26:6).[4]

As regards the *Hakafot* of Shemini Atzeret (in Israel) and Simḥat Torah (in the Diaspora), the Rema (1530–1572) writes in his supplementary notes for the Shulḥan Arukh: "It is our manner to withdraw all Torah Scrolls from the ark . . . to make *Hakafot* with them around the *bimah* [the raised platform in the synagogue] as was done previously with the *lulav* [during Sukkot]" (Rema, Oraḥ Ḥayyim 669:1).[5]

Three types of *Hakafot* are indicated: the *Arba Minim* around the *mizbe'aḥ* in Temple days, the *Arba Minim* around the *Sefer Torah* after the destruction of the Temple, and the *Sifrei Torah* around an empty *bimah* on Shemini Atzeret and Simḥat Torah.

We can appreciate encircling a *mizbe'aḥ* or a *Sefer Torah*, thereby acknowledging their centrality and holiness in Jewish life. But what is the significance of the *Sifrei Torah* encircling an empty center? The answer is that the center is not empty. God is symbolically there. When nobody is there, Someone is there. There is no place bereft of His Presence. The encircling *Sifrei Torah* pay homage to their Divine Author, acknowledging that the purpose of Torah is to direct us to God.

We intend to elaborate on three themes: the preeminence of the ethical, the *mitzvot* as the royal road to God, and the suggestive symbolism of the *Hakafot*.

The Preeminence of the Ethical

The verse informs us that a *mitzvah* which was made possible through a transgression is invalid. So decisive is this principle that even after the owner had given up any expectations of retrieving his *lulav* and had become resigned to the permanence of his loss, *yayush,* thus severing his ownership rights, the thief still cannot be accredited with the *mitzvah,* since he acquired it immorally (Suk. 30a; Maimon. Hil. Lulav 8:6).[6]

Besides its halakhic implications, the verse imparts a moral of major significance, reflecting the uniqueness of our faith. Cultic gods were not concerned with ethics. They were propitiated through hymns, sacrifices, orgies, and incantations, but not by charity, kindness, and truthfulness. Society may demand disciplined behavior for the purpose of social stability or patriotic cohesion, but the gods had no interest in such matters.

Judaism is unique in its insistence that "the Lord of Hosts is exalted through justice, and God the Holy One is sanctified through righteousness" (Isa. 6:15).[7] Only Abraham, with his faith in ethical monotheism, had the presumption to challenge God prior to the destruction of Sodom and Gomorrah. "Shall the whole world's Judge not act justly?" (Gen. 18:25).[8] It would never occur to a pagan to relate ethics to his deity.

The Difficult Ḥoshen Mishpat

Nonobservant Jews and Gentiles, too, are often heard to bemoan the hardships suffered by *shomrei mitzvot* whose lifestyles are constricted and depressed by ritual prescriptions and prohibitions. They accuse the Shulḥan Arukh of being stifling and oppressive, particularly in the areas of Sabbath and *kashrut* observance. Religious Jews, however, know that it is not torturous to abstain from golf or shopping one day of the week, and that, on the contrary, the Sabbath is a rare jewel of spiritual and physical delight, an *oneg Shabbat*. Similarly, *kashrut* restrictions may, at times, be inconvenient, especially while traveling, but dieting for various reasons is common to many groups.

The Shulḥan Arukh, the widely accepted Code of Jewish Law, is divided into four parts: the Oraḥ Ḥayyim—the daily round of religious observances, Sabbath, festivals, fasts, prayers, blessings, etc.; Yoreh De'ah—things forbidden and permitted, *issur v'hetter*, etc.; Even Ha'ezer—marriage, divorce, forbidden relationships, etc.; and the Ḥoshen Mishpat. To observe the teachings of the first three Orders is not difficult. In fact, it would be almost traumatic for anyone reared and schooled in a piously observant environment to deviate from a Torah way of life which is ideologically, morally, and emotionally appealing.

Rather, it is the Ḥoshen Mishpat, dealing with civil and

criminal law and all aspects of human relations, which is the most demanding and difficult to observe properly. While we relate to God with awe and submission in our ritual observances, we often allow our ego, greed, and lust to intervene and distort our value-judgments in dealing with our fellow man. The Hoshen Mishpat encompasses laws of litigation, partnerships, the collection of loans, damages, fraud, labor relations, personal injuries, and all manner of conducting business. Various types of explicit and implicit cheating and subliminally misleading advertisements are proscribed as being deceptive, *gonev da'at haberiyot.*

One who fulfills the Hoshen Mishpat scrupulously would find it considerably more difficult to become a millionaire, because of its restrictions on many popular money-making practices. It is the Hoshen Mishpat which reflects the essence of Judaism's greatness. The inspiring stories of the *Gedolim,* our foremost Sages, told to us for inspirational purposes by our parents and teachers, deal mostly with their unusual compassion and their sensitivity to the rights of others. It is primarily in the area of *bein adam lehavero,* interhuman relations, that Judaism is unique.

There are some who, though stringent in ritual observance, are less than meticulous in human relations. This, though inexcusable, may not be due to hypocrisy, but to the formidable standards of the Hoshen Mishpat with its demands that we discipline our greed in recognition of the rights and feelings of others. Even the *mitzvah* of *tzedakah,* to give charity, requires a readiness to lessen one's hard-earned equity for the sake of strangers, which is almost unnatural, and most find it difficult to observe properly.

And yet the Torah intertwines both the ritual and the ethical, and the Ten Commandments unite them in an indivisible entity, *bedibbur ehad* (Rashi, Ex. 20:1).[9] The Yiddish expression *ez iz shver tzu zein a Yid,* "it is difficult to be a Jew," is more appropriate, religiously speaking, in the ethical realm than in ritual observance.

It is a basic teaching of our faith that if you do not treat your fellow man properly, you are failing in your relationship with God. Also, if your ethics is not anchored in God, it will eventually be rationalized away, as is evidenced in our valueless secular society today. There must be a concurrence of ethics and ritual. For the Torah, a thief's prayer is no prayer; a stolen sacrifice is a wasted gesture. Unless your hands are washed, there is no point in encircling the altar.

Circling an Empty Center

We go around the *Sefer Torah* all of Sukkot, acknowledging its central importance in Jewish life. But on Shemini Atzeret and Simḥat Torah, we withdraw the *Sifrei Torah* to the periphery of the circle and march around the omnipresent Somebody who is at the center. From homage to the Torah all of Sukkot, we are now directed to God Himself.

There are modern Jews who, with genuine sensitivity and earnestness, are heard to ask, "We are looking to experience God and you give us a Shulḥan Arukh, telling us to daven, what not to eat, and how to conduct our marital lives. Why should we bog down in minutiae when we are searching for the infinite?"

Basically, the Torah is suspicious of subjective religiosity with its emphasis on transcendent fulfillment and its abandonment of physical reality as an irremediable vale of tears. Subjective religiosity is inherently self-centered and is concerned primarily with the salvation of the soul. Though it bemoans injustice, its focal point of concern and endeavor is not of this world.

The Halakhah insists that God be experienced out of a disciplined life which is hallowed and cleansed through the purifying influence of *mitzvot*. The Torah aspires to bring down the Divine Presence into the worldly arena of space and time, into the midst of earthly life. Not a flight to a higher world that is wholly good, but its mission is to superimpose, however imperfectly, the eternal world upon "them that dwell in houses of clay" (Job 4:19).[10] Rabbi Jacob taught: "Better is one hour of repentance and good deeds in this world than the whole of life in the world to come" (Av. 4:12).[11]

Holiness, in Judaism, refers to the sanctification of the earthly. "Rabbi Joshua b. Levi said: When Moses ascended on high, the ministering angels spoke before the Holy One, blessed be He, 'Sovereign of the Universe! What business has one born of woman among us?' He answered them, 'He has come to receive the Torah!' They said to Him, 'That sacred treasure . . . Thou desirest to give to flesh and blood?' The Holy One, blessed be He, said to Moses, 'Answer them yourself.' He then spoke before Him, 'Sovereign of the World! The Torah which Thou givest me, what is written therein?' 'I am the Lord thy God who brought thee out of the land of Egypt' [Ex. 20:2]. Said he to the angels, 'Did you go down to Egypt? Were you enslaved to Pharaoh?' etc. Again, 'what is written therein?' 'Honor thy father and mother' [Ex. 20:12]. 'Do you have any fathers and mothers?' Again, 'what is written therein?' 'Thou shalt not murder, thou shalt not commit adultery, thou shalt not steal' [20:13]. 'Is there jealousy among you; is the evil tempter among you?' Straightaway, the angels conceded to Moses" (Shab. 98b).[12]

The Torah is this-worldly; it is not for angels. We approach God through the totality of human existence, which relates the Jew to the physical world, to his fellow man, and simultaneously with God. There is no royal road to God; it is a long winding road up steep hills. Instantaneous devoutness which envelops the soul only is not the Torah way.

And so for seven days, we commit ourselves to the centrality of the Torah and Halakhah in our lives. And only then, on Shemini Atzeret and Simḥat Torah, does the Torah itself incline us towards that awesome Presence in the center of the circle.

The Suggestiveness of the Hakafot

The *Hakafot,* in circular movement, may suggest three concepts:

1. *All Jews Count.* During *Hakafot,* all marchers are equidis-

tant from the center, from God. One may be Rabbi Akiba, another the Gaon of Vilna, and the next humble "hewers of wood and drawers of water"—all have equal access to God. No person needs the intercession of others to approach Him. The doors of heaven will open before whoever devoutly knocks on its gates. "God is close to all who call upon Him, to all who call upon Him in truth" (Ps. 145:18).[13]

Our Sages taught: "Three crowns [distinctions] were bestowed upon Israel: the crown of Torah, the crown of priesthood, and the crown of royalty [Av. 4:17]. Aaron acquired the crown of priesthood. . . . David acquired the crown of royalty. . . . the crown of Torah, however, is ready and available for all Israel, for it is written, 'Moses commanded us a law, an inheritance of [all] the congregation of Jacob' [Deut. 33:4]" (Maimon., Hil. Talmud Torah 3:1; cf. Yoma 72 b).[14]

The *Arba Minim,* the Midrash teaches, illustrate the kinship and indispensability of all types of Jews. "Just as the *etrog* has taste as well as fragrance, so, too, does Israel have Jews who possess learning and good deeds, scholars and communal leaders; as the *lulav* has taste [the date of the palm tree] but not fragrance, so, too, do we have Jews who possess scholarship [acquired for self-serving reasons] but few good deeds; just as the *hadassim* [myrtle] have fragrance [myrtle was offered as incense] but no taste, so do those in Israel who practice good deeds but are unlearned; just as the *aravot* [willow] have neither taste nor fragrance, so, too, Israel has those who possess neither learning nor good deeds. What did the Holy One, blessed be He, do to those who are less than perfect? To destroy or dismiss them was impossible. He prescribed instead that all types be brought together in one band" (Lev. R. 30:11).[15] Only then, when they are together, is a blessing appropriate.

As He is equally accessible to all Jews, so should we be, in a spirit of *kiruv,* to those who, due to circumstances, have fallen out of the *Hakafot* circling the altar. An insular self-righteousness and indifference to the plight of those going their own way is indefensible. Only when all are bound together in a spirit of mutual concern is it a blessing for the Jewish people.

2. *The Ethics of Withdrawal.* When we circle, we simultaneously are drawn to the center even as we maintain our steady distance. Our journey forward is not thwarted, but it is deflected and inclined as by a magnetic pull in deference to an irresistible attraction. Such movement is similar to planetary and satellite travel in space.

In the *Hakafot,* we are drawn to the altar because the altar is a symbol of Judaism. As soon as Abraham arrived in Canaan, "he built an altar there and proclaimed the knowledge of the [true] God" (Gen. 12:8).[16] When he settled in Hebron and wherever he went, he built altars. Isaac did likewise (26:25), and so did Jacob (33:20, 35:7). At these altars the patriarchs preached the new faith, which is symbolically represented by the altar, namely, the lesson of sacrifice, the readiness to withdraw, to yield some aspects of one's freedom and indulgence in recognition of the Almighty, who is the source of all bounties.

The ethic of retreat or withdrawal is rooted in the kabbalistic mystery of *tzimtzum,* self-contraction, without which the creation of the world would have been impossible. The question is asked: Since God is infinite, encompassing all, how could God create a finite world extraneous to Himself? The Lurianic Kabbalah answers that God retreated in order to make room for a finite world. He (metaphorically) withdrew out of His love for man and for the world.

This doctrine of *tzimtzum* has moral relevance to man and is the foundation of our morality. If God withdrew, and creation is a result of His withdrawal, then, guided by the principle of *imitatio dei,* we are called upon to do the same. Jewish ethics, then, calls upon us, in certain situations, to engage in self-limitation and recoil from the full range of options available to us in life.

The Midrash informs us that it was Abraham who first used the Divine name *ADNY,* which recognized God as not only the Creator (*Elohim*) and Sustainer (*Havayah,* Tetragrammaton), but also as Master, the owner, the "lord of the manor" (Ber. 7:b).[17] This is explicit in the verse: "The earth and all its fullness belong to the Lord, the entire world and its inhabitants" (Ps. 24:1).[18] To exercise ownership implies the right to restrict or deny its use to others.

In general, the sacrifices asked of us are minimal. The Torah was not given to angels, and asceticism is not a Jewish way of life. Man is a natural being with desires which may legitimately be satisfied. But in his journey through life, he is asked to bend his course by relinquishing some small part of life's many options. Thereby, he will acknowledge the Source of all, Who is at the center of all existence. The table has been equated to an altar because at the table we eat, a biological activity, but we partake with dignity, with blessings, with permitted foods. We indulge in a full range of nourishment, but we withdraw on fast days and from particular foods. In a similar manner, all *mitzvot* prescribe and circumscribe; they do not stifle but deflect us to the altar, even as we move on our chosen path of life.

The concept of withdrawal is clearly manifest on the Sabbath. The Torah says: "You can work during the six workdays and do all your tasks. But on the seventh day is a Sabbath unto God, your Lord" (Ex. 20:8).[19] There is a positive allowance for a six-day period, but on the seventh to incline oneself towards the Center. This is the message of the altar of the patriarchs and of the *Hakafot* around the altar.

3. *Arrival and Departure.* In a circle, the point of departure is the point of arrival. We are always returning to the same place despite all our motion. In contrast, to travel in a straight line means to move further away from one's beginning.

To Jews, the past has remained intimately close. Abraham is not a mythical figure from the misty dawn of history. We cry annually with young Joseph, whose brothers conspired to throw him into a pit. The State of Israel, the central fact in modern Jewish history, came into being because even after nineteen hundred years of exile, the land of Israel continues to fascinate us. For centuries, on the ninth day of Ab, we sit on the ground

R. Moshe Hadarshan—91, 95, 101.
Mourning—60, 87f., 117ff., 125ff.

Naḥmanides—40, 43, 68, 93, 96, 97, 110, 111, 112.
Nazirite—102.
Nesuin—56.
Niḥum Avelim—122.
Nimrod—78.
Nineveh—141f.
Nishmat Kal Hai—147.
Noahide Laws—77, 80.

Or Haḥayyim—28.
Oved Elohim—95.

Parah Adumah—91, 94, 95, 100ff., 133.
Parashat Arayut—144, 146.
Particularism—146f.
Passover *Seder*—146f.
Patriarchic Covenant—66ff., 70, 72, 83, 86.
Pleasure principle—77f.
Prayer—48.
Prophecy—48.

Rav—126f.
Rashi—26, 27, 28, 30, 43, 76, 78, 88, 91, 101, 112, 113, 118, 150.
Rebecca—87.
Red Sea—111.
Rema—151.
Repentance—29, 125ff., 133ff., 141f., 154.
Reflections of the Rav, vol. 1—9.
Resurrection—123.
Revelation at Sinai—20, 48, 53, 66.
Ritual defilement—100, 103ff.; caused by death, 102.
Rosh Hashanah—143; *Musaf*—67.

Sabbath—152, 158.
Sarah—68, 74, 83ff.

Science, secular studies, and secular society—30, 41, 52, 58, 61, 92f., 145.
Sefer Haḥinnukh—128.
Sheloshim—128, 130.
Shema—18, 95, 118.
Shemini Atzeret—151, 154, 155.
Shetar hithayvut—66.
Sheva Berakhot—56ff.
Shilu'aḥ Hakan—96f.
Shivah—62, 120, 125ff.
R. Shneur Zalman of Lyady—96.
Shulḥan Arukh—152.
Simḥat Torah—151, 155.
Sinaitic Covenant—66ff., 74.
Sinfulness—127ff., 133, 138.
Sodom and Gomorrah—68, 75, 152.
Solomon—74, 84, 101.
Soloveitchik, Rav Joseph B.—9f.
Soloveitchik, Rav Moshe—9.
Subjective religiosity—154.
Sukkot—74, 150, 154, 159.

Taharah—133f., 139.
Tamei—103.
Taryag mitzvot—66.
Tefillin—26, 118.
Tekhelet—25ff.
Temple, destruction of—56, 150f., 159.
Ten Commandments—153.
Teshuvah—*See* Repentance.
Tetragrammaton—39, 50, 86, 157.
Tevillah—107ff., 133.
Tisha B'Av—111, 158.
Tumat-met—103, 104ff.
Tzaddik—95.
Tzelem Elohim—39, 84, 118, 129.
Tzimtzim—157.
Tzitzit—25ff.

Universal history—70.

Women's status in Judaism—85.

R. Yehudah (Judah) Hanassi—26,

32, 104ff.
R. Yoḥanan ben Zakkai—21, 102.
Yom Kippur—125, 127, 136ff.;
 Azazel ritual—94; *Ne'ilah*—
 121; Haftarah—137, 141ff.

Zechariah—73.
Zionism—71.